THE PSYCHOLOGY OF
FOREIGN LANGUAGE STUDY

The University of North Carolina Press, Chapel Hill, N. C.; The Baker and Taylor Company, New York; Oxford University Press, London; Maruzen-Kabushiki-Kaisha, Tokyo; Edward Evans & Sons, Ltd., Shanghai.

THE PSYCHOLOGY OF FOREIGN LANGUAGE STUDY

BY

H. R. HUSE
The University of North Carolina

CHAPEL HILL
THE UNIVERSITY OF NORTH CAROLINA PRESS
1931

Copyright, 1931, by
The University of North Carolina Press

PREFACE

The title of this work is intended to differentiate the present investigation from numerous essays on methodology and from manuals that give advice on a wide variety of topics based on personal, rather than scientific, induction.

The subject is the learning (memorizing) process, and what has been established on this point experimentally rather than rationally. Problems of curriculum, administration, classroom organization, and, generally, the art of teaching, are in no way concerned. The psychology of language, in an absolute sense, is not involved. Moreover, to use the valuable distinction made by Palmer, learning is considered only in its "studial aspect" and not in its "natural aspect." The problem that remains, namely the learning process, is, however, the one that concerns most vitally thousands of teachers and hundreds of thousands of students in the public schools.

Certain omissions in the list of the language experiments reviewed are explained by the restriction to studial learning of foreign languages, and by a necessary distinction between general statistical compilations and experiments in a more precise and particular sense.

Among many debts incurred, the author must mention particularly the report of the Canadian

Committee of the Modern Foreign Language Study, which has furnished much indispensable material, and both the published work and advice of Professor Coleman.

H. R. HUSE

Chapel Hill
April, 1931

CONTENTS

	PAGE
PREFACE	v
INTRODUCTION	3

PART I
THE EXPERIMENTAL FOUNDATIONS

I. DIRECT COMPARISONS BETWEEN METHODS...... 11
Clarahan, An Experimental Study—Bovée, "Some Fallacies of Formalism"—Pargment, Effect of Method—Other Experiments—Summary.

II. EXPERIMENTS RELATED TO METHODS........... 22
Kirkpatrick's Experiment—Peterson, Recall of Words, etc.—Schuyten, Vocabulary Arrangements—Libby, Sentences and Word Lists—Braunschausen, Direct Association—Netschajeff, Direct Association—Schlüter's Experiment—Schoenherr, Direct and Indirect Methods—Pohlmann's Experiment—Scholtkowska, Direct Method—Other Experiments—Summary.

III. EXPERIMENTS IN LEARNING AND RECALL....... 42
Mode of Presentation—Part and Whole Methods—Influence of Association (Context)—Complexity and Dissimilarity—Transfer and Interference—Variations in Memorial Capacity—Repetition versus Recall—Influence of Attitude—Distribution of Learning—Repetition, Drill—Organization of Material—Articulation—Effect of Rhythm—Position in a Series—Attention—Order of Presentation—Retroactive and Associative Inhibition—Effect of Age—Summary.

PART II
CURRENT PEDAGOGICAL DOCTRINES

IV. CURRENT PEDAGOGICAL DOCTRINES............ 81
Grammar—Paradigms—The Language Unit—Word Lists—The Influence of Context—Translation and Free Composition—The "Oral Approach"—Phonetics.

CONTENTS

PART III

AIMS AND METHODS—A BASIS FOR AN EXPERIMENTAL SCIENCE

V. METHODS AND OBJECTIVES 121
   The Dependence of Method—Multiplicity of Aims—Educational Value of Speaking Knowledge—Attainment of Speaking Knowledge—Effect of Bilingualism on Mental Development—The Direct Methods—Reading Knowledge.

VI. A SUMMARY OF THE SITUATION 149
   Experimental Results—The Current Doctrines—Methods and Objectives.

VII. A SUGGESTED BASIS FOR A SCIENCE OF LANGUAGE TEACHING 161

VIII. CERTAIN PROBLEMS AND IMPLICATIONS 166
   The Unit of Expression—Designation of the Units—Word Counts—The Use of Word Counts—Implications of the Restricted Program—The "Childlike Facility"—Combination of the Units—Some Suggested Experiments.

APPENDIX

EXPERIMENTS IN LEARNING WORD PAIRS 193
   1. The Relative Difficulty of Words. 2. Effect of Suggested Associations. 3. Organization of the Material. 4. Learning Units in Combination.

BIBLIOGRAPHY 214

INDEX 227

THE PSYCHOLOGY OF
FOREIGN LANGUAGE STUDY

INTRODUCTION

Few school subjects involve the interests of more individuals, are more written about, and with less agreement, than the subject of language study. Theories and methods for learning languages follow each other in almost endless succession, most of which claim some universal validity. Yet, in spite of the effort and discussion, teachers are divided into many camps, and even among members of a group, there is seldom an entire agreement.

The attempt here is to summarize the present knowledge concerning economical methods of language learning. This aim involves, first of all, a distinction between convictions based on general experience or on purely logical processes, and facts that have been established experimentally. Only experimental results offer a basis for assurance.

But in considering the experiments, a further limitation is necessary. In drawing conclusions from the evidence, there is room for subjective influences, and experiments cannot always be accepted at their face value. This is particularly so in the case of language experiments, which often are undertaken, not by disinterested parties, but by partisans of certain causes. The goal-idea may determine, if not the conclusions drawn, at least the particular results that reach the stage of publication. It has been necessary, therefore, to review these experiments in some detail, and to adopt a more critical attitude toward them than is found, for instance, in the similar work of Professor Handschin.

Professor Handschin's generous estimate of present experimental knowledge appears hardly confirmed by a close examination of the facts. The number of strictly language experiments has been very limited, the results often conflicting or uncertain, and the necessary conclusions largely negative. In the larger field of educational psychology, the situation is only slightly different. Although most experiments in that field have been performed under laboratory conditions and with adequate controls, on several of the most vital topics the results vary according to particular circumstances, and the total contribution that can be considered of immediate use to language teachers is, therefore, relatively slight.

The first part of this study is concerned with the experimental evidence. A second part examines current pedagogical doctrines to discover the unanimity or diversity of opinion. A third part considers aims and methods, but only in relation to their bearing on the learning process.

Several curious facts appear to be established by the evidence presented: (1) that the experimental study of language problems has hardly begun; (2) that opinions concerning grammar, paradigms, the language unit, word lists, etc., depend largely upon the varying connotations or implications of the terms used; and (3) that the aims of language study, with which methods and procedures are intimately bound up, are extremely diverse. These aims, estimates of values, or degrees of emphasis vary subjectively in each individual and provide almost numberless viewpoints from which the few facts and many theories may be regarded. The result is a certain anarchy both in doctrines and in practice.

Although the primary object here is to present the evidence concerning what is known, the question arises immediately as to whether it is possible to give scientific objectivity to the subject of language methodology, to eliminate the endless theorizing that may depend, in last analysis, upon the ambiguity of terms or on varying estimates of values. With this intent, a suggestion is hazarded which, if generally accepted, would afford a basis for a new applied science.

The possibility of such a reform would seem remote when one considers the antiquity of the problem. But certain recent developments are worth noting. The experimental approach to language problems dates back hardly twenty years. The first word counts, which involve a fundamental question, namely, what to teach, are very recent. Moreover, the Modern Language Study has marked a new development by redirecting the attention of leaders in the universities (whose sense of responsibility had somewhat wandered), to problems of a vital, immediate, and practical nature.

Apart from the present ambiguity of terms, the greatest difficulty in reaching a common basic understanding is the multiplicity of aims, nearly all of which may, in certain situations, be entirely legitimate. This variation in purposes affects both the kind of material to be presented and the way of presenting it, so that nearly any method may be good or bad according to the knowledge or discipline it is intended to impart. The attempt, as in the past, to find a universal panacea, a "new method" or formula, for accomplishing any and every aim, seems doomed to failure. Moreover, no general agreement can ever be reached as to single *ultimate* objective for all students, whose future careers and interests are obviously almost as varied as their faces. The hope is not in ultimate aspirations, but in finding, if possible, a common denominator, a minimum aim that will afford a beginning. If this is done, a simplification of the problem is at once possible. The task to be accomplished can be defined, not in the form of vague aspirations, but in terms of a concrete list of units of expression, established objectively by frequency of occurrence. In presenting this fixed amount of work, the criterion of economy of effort, which is a measurable quantity, offers a basis for experimental evaluations. With what to teach known and agreed upon, and with a criterion for evaluating various ways of presenting that material, the need for reasoning about immediate problems disappears, and language methodology can be transferred from the field of theoretical controversy to the laboratory.

There are, in the United States, over a million students studying foreign languages, both ancient and modern. In the lack of adequate experimental knowledge, the present methods and textbooks are based largely and necessarily on guesses and assumptions. When the guesses are wrong, thousands of innocent victims may suffer, who can protest only by punishing themselves through not learning. If many indications can be believed, that protest is not negligible. It is doubtful if educational psychologists and schools of education could find a more promising field for experimentation. The work done already in educational measurements has shown what accomplishment is possible when a concrete problem is defined, one that involves *measurable* quantities.

PART I
THE EXPERIMENTAL FOUNDATIONS

CHAPTER I

DIRECT COMPARISONS BETWEEN METHODS

Professor Handschin, in his *Methods of Teaching Modern Languages,* comments optimistically on the progress that has been made in the scientific investigation of language study. He states: "Upon a survey of the experiments in the economy of learning ... we ... find a number of important principles which we may consider as definitely settled; a number of others have been sufficiently established to give them the standing of high probability, and, until they are further proved or disproved, may be incorporated into pedagogical practice."[1]

Unfortunately, Professor Handschin does not review critically or in detail the experiments on which the principles are based. Many of these experiments admit of different interpretations, and the conclusions drawn by the experimenters may sometimes require qualification.

The purpose here is to review the language experiments more critically, in an attempt to discover what is certainly known, as contrasted with what is believed or generously assumed.

A first group of experiments attempt a direct comparison between complex methods or general

[1] P. 20.

procedures. As will be seen, certain difficulties are inherent in investigations of this kind.

§1

Clarahan, M., *An Experimental Study of the Methods of Teaching High School German,* University of Missouri Bulletin, Educational Series, Vol. I, No. 6, 1913.

The purpose of this experiment was to measure the relative value of the "grammar" method and the "reading" method. The distinction between these general procedures is stated as follows:

> Two methods were used, so that by comparison the advantages or disadvantages of either would be more evident. One was . . . a grammar method . . . because it gives the emphasis to grammar study. The other method may be called a reading method. . . . With both . . . there were the same underlying aims. The first aim was to attain the ability to read and understand with comparative ease simple, idiomatic German; to understand it when it is spoken; and to speak it with a good pronunciation. . . . The second aim was to secure a good foundation in German grammar.

> Five high school classes furnished the subjects of the experiment. The classes were as nearly uniform in size as possible. Three were reading sections, and two grammar sections. "No attempt was made to apportion the students as to age, ability, preparation and the like." "Teachers I, II, and IV were practice teachers, that is, they were teaching for the first time in preparation for their future work."

"As regards preparation . . . the teachers were probably about equal."

In the grammar sections, about five-sixths of the time was given to the study of grammar, and the remaining time to reading. In the reading sections, the proportions of grammar and reading were reversed.

A conclusion affirming the superiority of the reading method is based on the results of a final examination (old type) which showed a combined average of 62 per cent for one group and 63 per cent for the other. A reading test for pronunciation showed a difference of 6 per cent in favor of the reading groups, obtained by rather complicated computations.

The essential facts of the experiment are presented very fully and objectively. The conclusion, however, demands considerable qualification. In every class conducted over a period of months, there are almost numberless factors that influence the attainment. The importance of the teacher and of the particular pupils in the coöperative effort makes the method used only a secondary factor. The results here, however, are remarkably insignificant. Two classes that differ in attainment by only 1 per cent are, for all practical purposes, exactly alike. In any case, it would be impossible to attribute a difference to any one factor to the exclusion of the others.

Professor Handschin cites the conclusion of this experiment as one of the points definitely established:

> The reading method is superior to the grammar-translation method for assimilating reading texts as well as for assimilating grammatical knowledge.[2]

In the bibliographical notes of the report of the Canadian Committee of the Modern Foreign Language Study, the following note occurs:

> An attempt was made to control variable factors, but the experiment should be repeated with larger numbers and more modern and precise methods of control. The study is interesting as one of the earliest objective experiments of language teaching methods.[3]

Concerning the oral reading test, Professor Coleman points out that since the experimental sections had more practice in reading, it is not surprising that they excelled.[4]

§2

Bovée, A. G., "Some Fallacies of Formalism," *Modern Language Journal*, 1923, pp. 131-44.

This study compares the grammar method and the direct method in relation to reading ability and grammatical knowledge. Two classes in two high

---

[2] *Op. cit.*, p. 46.
[3] *Modern Language Instruction in Canada*, I, 251.
[4] *The Teaching of Modern Foreign Languages in the United States, Publications of the American and Canadian Committees of the Modern Foreign Language Study*, XII, 155.

schools furnished the subjects for the immediate comparison. The relative attainment of the groups was measured by an examination. The conclusion indicates the superiority of the direct method.

Few details are given concerning this investigation. In respect to the purpose, the experimenter states that "the grammar method reposes on the unproved assumption that the more of this type of work we do, the better the pupils read. This is precisely the fallacy I am seeking to establish. . . ."

The tests for attainment were prepared with great care. The author points out that "it would be presumptuous to make any extensive claims on such meager data," but adds that "the results become highly significant when considered with a study of ability in Latin in secondary schools conducted by Prof. H. A. Brown in the schools of . . . New Hampshire."

From a critical viewpoint, the only conclusion that can be drawn is that one school was better than the other, as judged by the tests used. It is quite possible that this difference was due to the methods of instruction, but it would require a large amount of statistical data to give that assumption importance or validity.

§3

Pargment, M. S., "The Effect on Achievement of the Method Used," *Modern Language Journal*, 1927, pp. 502-12.

This elaborate and careful experiment which attempts to measure the results of extreme forms of the direct and grammar methods has received a considerable amount of favorable mention.

Four beginning French classes were given nearly identical conditions as to teacher, hour, size of class. A "pure direct" and "grammar-translation" method were used. The instructors were equally opposed to the two methods; they were in favor of a "modified" direct method. One instructor taught two classes, one by each method.

An attempt was made to apply extreme forms of both procedures. "However ... we taught the students how to pronounce, and gave them some practice in reading aloud and in listening to spoken French. We did this because we did not think that the possible good that may come out of our experiment would justify the certain handicapping of half a hundred young men and women which, in our opinion, would follow a strict application of the grammar-translation method."

The conclusions are as follows: (1) "Method has an effect on achievement." (2) "The pure direct method cannot be successfully used in a two-year course unless we wilfully sacrifice the most important aspect of language—an intelligent reading knowledge."

The conclusions are certainly carefully guarded. The first, namely, that "method has an effect on achievement," could scarcely be disputed; the great problem, however, is to isolate the effect of method from dozens of other factors. The second conclusion is of considerable interest; but it would doubtless be difficult to find any partisans of either method who would approve of the particular forms in which they were administered.

* * * * * * * * * * *

Two other studies will be mentioned briefly:

Prof. Boveé in an additional experiment, compares reading ability in French and English, using a French reading test, similar to the Thorndike-McCall English text in order to measure the results. One purpose of the experiment was to show the rôle of oral work, and, in the experimental class, the oral work was reduced to a minimum and the main "appeal" was "to the eye." The experimenter mentions that some have doubted the validity of the test, but cites an opinion in its support. The conclusion is as follows: "It would seem, first of all, that if our objective is to teach the pupils to read, then the thing to do is to make them read as much as possible. Yet, if we push them ahead too far, and neglect oral practice, we do not do our work solidly, for it does not stay, as is indicated by our experience with the first class. Second, the larger ingredient of oral practice seems to have had the effect of so drilling the material that it established the reading adaptation on a firmer basis, with the result that there was a greater permanency to the ability attained, as proved by the fact that nobody went backwards and 85 per cent went forward in the second class. Obviously, these statistics dealing with classes of students averaging from 30 to 45 have not a convincing value, and yet they have a fair significance, and may be indicative of a deep and underlying truth."[5]

An experiment in learning Spanish has been reported by Greenup and Segel.[6] In an experimental group grammatical forms were discussed only when brought up by the students themselves. In the control group, "an effort was made to follow the program of the average Spanish teacher." The summary is as follows: "Two groups of beginning junior college Spanish students, equated fairly well for general academic ability and for initial performance in Spanish, were subjected to two different procedures for a period of four and a half months. The one group —the control group—was taught by the usual grammar-translation method, together with a certain amount of reading and conversation. The other group—the experimental group—was taught a little grammar at the very beginning, and then shifted into a reading and conversational method where grammar was incidental and brought up only on occasion." . . . The results were in favor of the experimental group.

SUMMARY

Experiments intended to evaluate "methods" as a whole by comparison of results in a few classes or in different institutions are necessarily inconclusive. Only a very large amount of similar statistical data

---

[5] "An Indicated Effect of Oral Practice," *Modern Language Journal*, 1928, pp. 178-82.

[6] "An Experimental Study of the Relation between Methods and Outcomes in Spanish Instruction," *Mod. Lang. Jour.*, 1929, pp. 208-12.

could be in any way conclusive. Incidentally, this statistical information has been furnished by the nation-wide investigation of the Modern Foreign Language Study, which reaches no conclusion in favor of any "method." Experiments of this kind usually confirm some belief, or else fail to reach the stage of publication.

The method itself is only one factor in the attainment; the teacher, the amount of work imposed and accomplished by the students, the effect of competing subjects, the varied circumstances of the teachers' and pupils' history and experience—these, and a multitude of other factors, enter into the final results. It is a truism that a good teacher can succeed with any method, and likewise, much depends on the particular students. A good application of a poor method might easily secure better results than a poor application of a good method. A method exists, moreover, only in relation to a purpose, and a procedure good by one criterion might be poor by another. The terms used such as "grammar-translation" method, or "reading" method have different meanings, implications or connotations to different individuals—both the direct and grammar methods are complex wholes, with infinite shades and variations. Except as a general classification, meaningless in precise experimentation, the "method" does not exist. When reduced to a concrete reality, it becomes this textbook or that, or some particular procedure or technique.⁷

In this conection, the Canadian Committee of the Modern Foreign Language Study, remark:

1. Ticknor, Judd and others are correct in asserting that there is no one best method; the method to be used varies with the skill and interest of the teacher, the age of the pupils, the linguistic surroundings in which learning is proceeding, and so forth. . . . The claims for a universal superiority of any method are matters of faith, rather than of evidence.

2. No one method as used by teachers of language is 'pure,' i.e., the distinction between methods tends in practice to break down. This mixing of methods may be done either by the pupil or the teacher or by both.

3. The results secured vary according to the type of test applied; according to the period of learning that has preceded; and, without doubt, according to the method of teaching and learning to which the

---

[7] Bagster-Collins, in giving an account of the history of modern language instruction, perceives this difficulty at once. He states: "A clearer and, on the whole, more accurate picture of modern language teaching during the greater part of the 19th century can be obtained from a study of the textbooks most in demand in their day than from the existing scattered accounts of method." *Publications of the Modern Language Study*, XVII, 79.

Professor Cheydleur in a study published in the *French Review*, January, 1931, follows the same line of attack. Instead of experimenting with methods as abstract principles, he chooses for comparison certain definite textbooks, and his study provides, therefore, valid and useful statistical data.

subjects were accustomed before the experiment was undertaken.[8]

Professor Coleman, summarizing the evidence, states:

Despite a certain amount of experimentation . . . there is little concrete and wholly trustworthy evidence to show to what extent a given classroom method is, in itself, productive of superior or of inferior results.[9]

[8] *Modern Language Instruction in Canada,* I, 63.
[9] *The Teaching of Modern Foreign Languages in the United States,* p. 276.

CHAPTER II

EXPERIMENTS RELATED TO METHODS

Certain experiments listed under this heading belong to the classification only by virtue of having been cited frequently by writers on methods; others relate very directly to problems of language study.

§1

Kirkpatrick, E. A., "An Experimental Study of Memory," *Psy. Rev.*, 1894, pp. 602-09.

This experiment is frequently cited in support of a direct method. Professor Handschin mentions it together with certain other studies as a basis for another "established principle," i.e., that memory for objects or movements is greater than for verbal impressions.[1]

The subjects were pupils in a "typical" school and college in all grades from the third primary up. Three lists of words were prepared, one of which was presented orally, another written on the board, and for the third list, the objects themselves were shown. The words of the second list which had previously been written on the board were uncovered one by one and rubbed out at the same rate as the first list was read.

Additional lists contained names of concrete objects, verbs representing sounds such as "hiss," "splash," "whiz," etc., and adjectives and verbs such as "black,"

[1] *Op. cit.*, p. 45.

"sparkle," "gloom," etc. The pupils were asked to think of the objects named in the first list, of the sound of the second, and of the visual appearance of the third list. Concerning the control of the experiment, the author remarks: "How closely they [the pupils] followed these directions, it is impossible to say, but their faces indicated that they were trying to do so." The equivalent difficulty of the lists was tested in one class by inverting the method of presenting certain series.

Tests for retention after three days showed remarkable results. "Probably the most enthusiastic advocate of object teaching would hardly have dared assert that if the names of ten common objects were pronounced to and written by pupils they would after three days remember but one-seventh as many of them as they would if they were allowed to look at each of the objects a fraction over a second and write the names, yet the numbers .91 and 6.29 [taken from a table of the returns] indicate that such would be the result."

A curious fact about this experiment is that it has almost no connection with foreign language teaching. The problem was merely the retention of a series, without association between objects or native words, and foreign words.

§2

Peterson, H. A., "Recall of Words, Objects and Movements," *Psy. Rev. Mon. Supp.*, No. 17, 1903, pp. 207-33.

The problem here, as in several later studies, was to determine the economy of associating foreign words with native words or directly with objects or movements. The materials were numbers, nonsense words, and vernacular words paired with foreign words or associated with objects or movements. Six adults served as subjects under controlled laboratory conditions. The conclusion favored the object method of presentation, but with certain necessary qualifications.

The experiments were in four series. In the first, the "A" set, numbers were paired with nouns, with objects, with verbs, and with movements. The "B" set contained nonsense words paired as above. In the "C" set, the verbs were dissyllabic words; the nouns and objects (i.e., their verbal equivalents) were monosyllabic, as before. The movements in this series employed objects instead of being merely movements of the body. The "D" set consisted of a few series of nouns, objects, verbs, and movements dissociated from foreign symbols, to test memory for words, objects, or movements presented in simple series.

In series "A" (numbers paired with nouns, objects, verbs, and movements) the results showed a superiority both in immediate and delayed recall for numbers that were related to objects and to movements.

In the "B" series (nonsense words, paired as above), which is of particular interest, the results were as follows for recall after two days:

Subject	Nouns	Objects	Verbs	Movements
M	54%	62%	63%	61%
S	8	21	7	12
Hu	11	30	5	59
Ho	33	30	17	58
B	19	57	13	27
Mo	57	94	13	85
(average)	30	49	20	50

In the "C" set, the average gain in the object pairs was 22 per cent; in the movement pairs, 36 per cent. In recall after nine and sixteen days "The most interesting fact which developed was an apparently slower rate of forgetting in many cases of the nouns and verbs than of the objects and movements."

The "D" set tested merely the ability to recall familiar words, objects and movements. Four subjects recalled objects better than nouns and movements better than verbs.

In interpreting the results, it should be noted that the experimenter excluded all cases of recall due to indirect associations, which he recognizes as the most powerful factor in recall.

The conclusion is as follows: (1) "That those five subjects who recall objects better than nouns (involving images) when each occurs alone, also recall objects better than nouns when each is recalled by means of an unfamiliar verbal symbol with which it has been coupled, (2) that the same is true of verbs and movements...."

In reference to the indirect associations, the experimenter states: "We see ... that the likelihood of recalling couplets in which indirect associations did not occur in learning is 63 per cent after one day, and that there is a diminution of 44 per cent in the next fifteen days. The fall is greatest during the second day. On the other hand, the likelihood of recalling couplets in which indirect associations did occur is 82 per cent after one day, and there is a diminution of only 18 per cent during the next fifteen days.

"It is evident, then, that in all investigations dealing with language material, the factor of indirect associations —a largely accidental factor affecting varying amounts of the total material—is by far the most influential of all the factors, and any investigations which have heretofore failed to isolate it, are not conclusive as to the other factors."

No very broad generalizations concerning language teaching can be based on these results, since in addition to the effect of indirect associations which, practically, are very important, the only objects and movements involved were simple, concrete objects, and very simple movements. With more complicated materials, the advantage in favor of the object-movement presentation might disappear.[2]

§3

Schuyten, M. C., "Experimentelles zum Studium der gebräuchlichsten Methoden im Fremdsprachlichen Unterricht," *Zeit. f. Exp. Pädagogik*, 3 Bd., 1906.

[2] For an extensive review of this experiment, see Schlüter, L., in *Zeit. f. Psychol.*, 1914, pp. 13-17.

This experiment attempted to measure the relative value of various vocabulary arrangements.

A first preliminary investigation used the experimenter's twelve-year-old daughter as the subject. Later the results were confirmed by repeating the experiment in two girls' and two mixed schools. The procedure was to write on the blackboard lists of French words with their vernacular equivalents in the following order: Foreign word, Native word; then to cover up one column in order to test retention. The same experiment was repeated with English words instead of French words. The results favored the Foreign-Word—Native-Word arrangement. The author believes that attention is more firmly aroused by presenting first the foreign word, and that the form of the word is consequently better imprinted on the mind.

§4

Libby, W., "An Experiment in Learning a Foreign Language," *Ped. Sem.*, 1910, pp. 81-96.

This study proposed to measure the memory for isolated words as compared with memory for sentences in the foreign tongue. The materials consisted of Italian word lists, presented to a college class of ten students. The conclusion favors the method of presenting words in sentences rather than in word lists.

Some of the sentences used were as follows: "Il treno è in ritardo; La supplico di non abbandonarmi, etc." Words: legare, edizione, ponderato, sarta, mosca, mano, lato, etc.

Various remarks of students are noted which may serve to indicate the difficulties of classroom experimentation generally. "D., as she said, waked up toward the end of the twenty minutes to the fact that a test in memory was in progress ... and applied her attention with characteristic energy to the translation." "E., as she later recognized, was greatly aided in translation by a special ability to associate the parts of the English equivalent. She wrote 'In translation, if I could remember what one or two words meant, I could recall the translation of the entire sentence.'"

The general conclusion of the experimenter is a recommendation for more experimentation. "... our study leads us to sympathize fully with the humorous appeal, in reference to method, of one of the best students: 'Give me liberty or give me death!'"

This experiment, to which the experimenter appears to attach relatively slight importance, has been cited frequently in support of the doctrine that "new words must be presented in context."[3]

§5

Braunschausen, N., "Les méthodes d'enseignement des langues étrangères," *Revue Psychol.*, Vol. 3 (1910).

Working on the same problem as Peterson, Braunschausen likewise found that associating for-

[3] Notably by Handschin, *op. cit.*, pp. 39, 46., and in *Modern Language Instruction in Canada*, I, 59.

eign words with objects produces better results than associating them with vernacular words.

The materials were Latin words which would occur later in the course, but which, at the time of the experiment were unknown to the pupils. In a preliminary test, these words were pronounced, then written on the blackboard in three series of five words, Latin-German, German-Latin, and object-Latin (the object presumably pictured). The results showed first an advantage in favor of the Latin-German arrangement, but this result was discovered to be due to the position of that arrangement in the series. Later experiments gave better results for the Object-Latin series. The second best arrangement appeared to be the vernacular word—foreign word. Tests were both for immediate and delayed recall. One class in a gymnasium offered all the subjects.

§6

Netschajeff, A., "Psychol. Beobachtungen zur Frage über den Fremdländischen Sprachunterricht," *Psychol. Studien,* Vol. IX, Nos. 1 and 2, 1908.

As in the Braunschausen experiment, the purpose of this investigation was to measure the relative value of associating foreign words with objects or with vernacular words. Netschajeff found that memory for foreign words paired with vernacular words is superior to memory for foreign words associated with objects. Forty adults served as subjects under laboratory conditions.

This experiment was carried out under the direction of Prof. Netschajeff in the psychological laboratory at St. Petersburg. The materials consisted of artificial words of equivalent length and difficulty, presented on the apparatus of Müller. The subjects read aloud the words shown, which were displayed in four series, 1. vernacular word—foreign word, 2. foreign word—vernacular word, 3. object—foreign word, and 4. foreign word—object.

The results showed that an average of 103 seconds were required for learning paired words, whereas 122.55 seconds were required for the word-object series. In delayed recall (115-123 days) 44 per cent of the words presented in the first manner were remembered; 35.19 per cent of the words that had been associated with objects. The experimenters found also that there was less fatigue in learning the verbal equivalents.

§7

Schlüter, L., Experimentelle Beiträge zur Prüfung der Anschauungs und der Uebersetzungs Methode bei der Einführung in einen fremdsprachlichen Wortschatz," *Zeit. f. Psych.*, 1914, pp. 1-114.

This experiment was begun in the winter of 1910-1911 and ended in the summer of 1912. It is probably the most thorough experimental investigation that has been made to determine the relative advantage of different methods of instruction.

The report of the experimental results gives a review and criticism of the previous experiments, notably those of Peterson, Schuyten, Braunschausen and Netschajeff, and an historical sketch of the various methods of language teaching.

The particular problem for investigation was the relative merits of associating word and word, and word and object. Both the presentations of the material to be learned and the tests for recall were according to the various arrangements, i.e., foreign word first, native word first, the object first (in case of recall), and so on. Other subjects investigated were the tendency to think of the vernacular word when an object was presented, the influence of position in a series, the mnemonic aids used by the students in learning the lists, etc. Tests for retention were made in most cases after twenty-four hours. A number of conclusions are given, the principal of which are as follows: The relative value of the particular arrangement in the presentation depends upon whether reproduction knowledge or recognition knowledge is demanded. If the native word must be recalled, the arrangement, foreign word—native word, is more effective, but if the stimulus is the object or the native word, the arrangement, object—foreign word, is more effective. Concerning the value of object presentation vs. native word, no one method showed a very clear superiority. The experimenter points out, moreover, that neither method of *presentation* insures the same method of *learning*. When an object is presented, the subject tends to think of a vernacular word, and, in the same way, when word pairs are presented, the object often comes to mind. In about 70 per cent of the cases, the vernacular word was suggested by the direct method which endeavored to eliminate it.

§8

Schoenherr, W., *Direkte und Indirekte Methode im Neusprachlichen Unterricht.* Leipzig, Quelle and Meyer, 1915. 83 pp.

The account of this experiment is based on the review contained in the report of the Canadian Committee of the Foreign Language Study.[4]

The purpose of this experiment was to test direct and indirect methods of vocabulary presentation. The subjects (two classes of boys) were divided into two groups, apparently of equal ability. The students in the direct method group had lists of French words associated with pictures; the other group used lists of words with their German equivalents. The pupils studied the lists until they considered themselves ready to recite, and the time required was noted. The tests for retention were made in various ways, e.g., the French word, the German word, or the object was used as the stimulus. The results show a considerable advantage of the direct method in the amount retained, but the direct method pupils required more time in the early series. It should be noted that the subjects were children only eight or nine years old.

[4] *Modern Language Instruction in Canada*, I, 131-34.

§9

Pohlmann, A., *Experimentelle Beiträge zur Lehre vom Gedächtnis*, Berlin, 1906.

This experiment tested the effect of various methods of presenting different kinds of materials including words. The subjects were five classes in boys' and girls' schools, ages, nine to fourteen. The experimenter concludes that oral presentation of meaningful words is better than visual; visual better than oral in the case of meaningless words.

Three different investigations were involved in this experiment: (1) to determine the relative difficulty of different classes of materials, (2) to test the influence of place associations (arrangements), and (3) to measure the influence of the method of presentation in the case of varied materials. The outline given above relates only to the part of the experiment dealing with words and nonsense syllables. Besides the conclusion stated above, other points mentioned are that concrete objects are recalled better than words, and that simple methods of presentation are more effective than combined methods.

§10

Scholtkowska, Gita, "Experimentelle Beiträge zur Frage der direkten und der indirekten Methode im Neusprachlichen Unterricht," *Zeit. f. Angew. Psych.*, 1925, pp. 65-87.

As in previous experiments the attempt here was to determine the relative advantages of direct and indirect methods of vocabulary presentation. An artificial language provided the materials. The subjects were two classes of fifteen pupils, twelve to thirteen years old. Scholtkowska found that in the initial stages of learning the direct method was more advantageous for her subjects; later the indirect method was superior.

The report of this experiment points out that the experiments of Peterson, Netschajeff, Braunschausen, Schlücter and Schoenherr dealt merely with isolated words. In this study, *sentences* containing various kinds of words were used for purposes of comparison. The ultimate purpose was to determine by more nearly approximating actual conditions whether the direct or indirect method is more advantageous for beginning instruction.

The artificial language constructed was extremely simple. Only words of one syllable were used, and without inflection of the nouns or articles. The verbs were used only in the 3d person singular. In the direct method class, the objects represented by the nouns were pointed out, and the movements expressed by the verbs were likewise indicated without use of the mother tongue. In the indirect method class, the words and sentences were translated. The results showed different relative attainments with different kinds of materials. The memory for concrete nouns, and the immediate recall of prepositions and verbs showed an advantage in favor of the direct method, but in learning nouns in adverbial combinations, in delayed recall of prepositions and verbs, and free formation of new sentences, the results were in favor of the indirect method. The final conclusion is that the direct method is more advantageous for children in beginning their study, but that this advantage disappears later.

* * * * * * * * * * * *

In addition to the experiments reviewed above, three other studies may be mentioned.

An investigation by Professor Buswell[5] represents an extremely elaborate and carefully controlled study of eye movements of students of various ages and attainments, in reading passages in foreign languages. On the basis of the eye movements observed, a conclusion is drawn in favor of a direct method. There is a striking difference, however, in the procedure here and that followed in the equally careful experiments of Schlüter, Pohlmann, and Scholtkowska. The latter endeavored to discover some fundamental and essential difference between the two general methods of language study, to isolate that factor, and by a careful comparison of results obtained by controlled study under similar conditions, but with different methods, to make some general conclusions as to the relative advantages of the methods involved. Their experiments involved controlling conditions rigorously in respect to a small point directly related to the teaching and learning process. In the case of Professor Buswell's experiment, however, a resultant condition was investigated primarily, namely, the character of the eye movements and the comprehension

---

[5] *A Laboratory Study of Reading of Modern Foreign Languages.* Vol. II, *Publications of the American and Canadian Committees on Modern Languages.*

of different groups of students from schools taught by different methods. In final analysis, granting the effectiveness of a study of eye movements as a criterion for attainment, the investigation amounted to a mere examination. To attribute the superiority of one group over another (14 students only served as one term for the comparison) to the direct or indirect method, rather than to some hundred other possible factors, seems entirely unwarranted. This is especially so, inasmuch as the "direct method" involved, as the introduction to the report of the experiment by the Modern Foreign Language Committee points out, is not the direct method as universally understood, and since, as has been mentioned, the term "method" is largely meaningless anyway, except in terms of particular procedures, textbooks, teachers, and students.[6]

[6] To review this experiment adequately would require more space than is available. In testing vernacular reading, the procedure adopted is probably useful, but, in the case of foreign languages, other measures exist. Eye-movements, good or bad, appear somewhat irrelevant when what counts is an end-result that can be measured in terms of time and understanding.

Here are some of the delicate and elusive variables involved: the young student who understands almost nothing races along with few fixations and few regressions; later, with a beginning of understanding, the fixations increase; then later, with more mature habits, they again decrease. But all this depends upon what is read. Nothing is solid or fixed for anyone. The mature reader has one set of fixations in reading his newspaper, and another in reading a legal contract. Likewise the child, through variable factors in individual experience, may have more trouble with one passage than with another. A failure to grasp some key word or phrase may qualify the total performance, as also, of course, the degree of comprehension, and the state of mind. The difficulty of equating passages would require a procedure as delicate as the technique for measuring eye movements. Comprehension, also, is a very subtle matter. Accuracy may count more

An experiment by Robert D. Cole[7] at the Lawrenceville, N. J., High School compared the results obtained in ability to write French by teaching according to the grammar-translation method and by the "free-translation" method. The differences in attainment of two groups showed an advantage in favor of the "free translation" method, but the difference was slight, and the experimenter points out that "in all cases the number of students was extremely small, and the methods of testing limited, so that the results are more in the nature of a tendency than a proved conclusion."

than the style of the performance. Everyone is familiar with very fluent misreadings of the simplest directions. In this experiment the measurement of style was minute and delicate, of comprehension, rough and secondary. When to this are added the factors that determine classroom efficiency, the personality, energy, industry, temperament, etc., of the teachers and pupils, the difficulty of concluding concerning method becomes obvious. Moreover, the "direct reading method" found most effective, represents a desirable and attainable end, but as a *method* in beginning study, the "direct association of the foreign expression and the meaning" almost certainly involves a psychological impossibility. If the analysis of Palmer and the experiments of Schlüter can be believed, the most ingenious devices for direct association lead inevitably, not to an independent concept, but to a vernacular word that represents the concept. On this point see pages 93-94, 182 ff.

A section of Professor Coleman's report (*op. cit.*, 171 ff.) shows the striking variations in attainment in a large number of schools where the same method is used, including, incidentally, one of the schools that offered subjects for Professor Buswell's report. Even within the same school, and with the same method, extreme variations in attainment may occur. In the light of Professor Coleman's comparison of achievement, the impossibility of concluding concerning method by measuring relative attainment in a few instances, and without isolating the effect of method alone, becomes an established fact.

[7] "Free Composition vs. Translation in Developing Ability to Write a Foreign Language," *Mod., Lang. Jour.*, 1927, 200-206.

An experiment reported by Grinstead[8] compares the results obtained by one subject (a fifteen-year-old boy) in learning words by looking up their meanings in the dictionary as encountered in reading, and in learning words presented in lists, looking up their meanings in the same way. The gain for the context method was 3 per cent on the second presentation. The lists of words and detailed results are not shown in the report of this experiment. A more practical test would have presented the isolated words paired with their equivalents, since word lists seldom appear in any other form.

SUMMARY

The results of experiments to determine the relative value of direct and of indirect methods are largely inconclusive. The experiment of Kirkpatrick has no direct relation to the problem, since it involved memory for words and objects detached from foreign language material. It is mentioned only because the results have been interpreted as giving weight to the theory that the direct association of the foreign symbol and the object is advantageous.[9]

The experiments of Peterson, Netschajeff, Schlüter, Braunschausen, Schoenherr and Scholtkowska all relate directly to the problem of vocabulary presentation, and more particularly to the relative

---

[8] "An Experiment in the Learning of Foreign Words," *Jour. Ed. Psy.*, 1915, VI, 242-45.

[9] Cited by Handschin, *op. cit.*, p. 45.

value of associating words with words, or words with objects or movements. The findings are somewhat diverse, but the experiments are far from being equally well controlled and equally significant. The Peterson experiment, for special reasons, excluded all cases of recall that were due to indirect associations, a procedure which affected considerably the total results. After an extensive review of this experiment, Schlüter concludes that it is not satisfactory in respect to exactness and completeness.[10] A distinction is necessary between casual class experiments and more extensive investigations conducted according to strict laboratory procedures. The work of Schlüter is monumental in comparison with several other experiments (notably those of Braunschausen and of Kirkpatrick), and an interpretation of the results would need to give added weight to her conclusions.

Leaving aside the question of method, these facts appear to have been established experimentally:

1. In the case of children, there is economy in associating simple concrete objects directly with foreign words, but this economy may disappear in the case of adults. Moreover, the method of presentation does not insure necessarily a presupposed method of learning, since, when objects are presented, a large proportion of subjects will associate the foreign word, not with the object, but with the

[10] *Op. cit.*, pp. 13-17.

object's vernacular equivalent, and the reverse process occurs when vernacular words are substituted for the objects.

2. The evidence concerning the advantage of placing the vernacular word first or last is conflicting and inconclusive, but it would appear from Schlüter's experiment that the native word should come first if the intent is to insure better reproduction knowledge, the foreign word first for recognition knowledge.

3. While most of the experiments involved only individual words, the results obtained by Scholtkowska indicate that no very striking differences are likely when various classes of words are used or complete sentences.

It should be noted that these experiments used only very simple and readily understandable materials. It is quite possible that a drawing of a very simple object might serve as well as or better than its vernacular equivalent, to convey and impress the meaning of the foreign word, but the situation might be very different in presenting less easily portrayed materials. The practical possibilities of the object method are limited, therefore, by the proportion of words in a given vocabulary that would admit of this treatment.

The experiments not included in the above summary have a certain statistical value, but are hardly extensive or thorough enough to permit conclusions

RELATED EXPERIMENTS

without further confirmation. This fact is pointed out in certain cases by the experimenters themselves.[11] One principle that Professor Handschin mentions as having been definitely established, namely, that learning words in sentences is easier for immediate or deferred recall than learning isolated words, is based on the experiments of Libby, Grinstead, and Binet and Henri. The Binet and Henri experiment, which is mentioned later (see p. 69) has little to do with learning foreign languages; the Grinstead experiment, reported without details in three pages, was based on observing the work of one fifteen-year-old subject for a period of ten days, and the Libby experiment involved the ability to remember a complete thought when several clues are given, e.g., *il treno* (a key word) *è in ritardo*. The Canadian Committee recognizes the inconclusiveness of this experiment "because of failure to control incentives or relative difficulties of the subject matter used."[12]

---

[11] Libby, see p. 27; Cole, see *supra*, p. 37.
[12] *Modern Language Instruction in Canada*, I, 316.

CHAPTER III

EXPERIMENTS IN LEARNING AND RECALL

The vast number of investigations of learning and recall make a selection both of topics and of particular experiments necessary. Here the basis of selection has been, in general, the degree of relationship to concrete present problems of language teaching, or to various points involved in discussions of language methodology. A critical consideration of certain statements about established principles, such as is contained in Professor Handschin's book, suggests that it is safer to err on the side of omission than inclusion. For instance, a number of experiments on tuition, on positive and negative transfer, on affective tone, interpolated activities, etc., would be important to the writer of language texts if absolute trust could be placed in the universal validity of the laws established. But, in many cases, such laws are based on few and recent experiments, with particular materials, and a small number of subjects. It happens occasionally that results depend upon the method of scoring used, i.e., whether in terms of time, relearning, or what not. In a few cases, notably "mode of presentation" and "part and whole" methods, the results of many experimenters are so conflicting that the only significant fact is the uncertainty of generalization, and the need for extreme caution.

In the following account, conclusions based on verbal materials mainly have been considered, and especially those experiments that deal with paired associates. Serial learning of verbal material is not directly related to problems of foreign language study. Conclusions based on animal learning, maze problems, the acquisition of various types of skills, etc., have also been omitted except in a few cases where they offer confirmation of other experiments, or throw some light on different ways of interpreting results. A purely formal and objective principal of choice was not possible.

The classification of the experiments does not follow in all cases the one used most generally by psychologists because of certain differences in the terminology used in language discussion. For instance, "context" has a different sense in psychology and in language pedagogy, and it has appeared less confusing to class experiments in that field under "association" or "complexity and dissimilarity." Other differences in classification are apparent.

The rather distinct problems of learning, retention and recall have not been separated in the following summary. It is unlikely that in the present stage of experimental knowledge of foreign language learning, any serious confusion will result.

On topics which involve no very fundamental or controversial questions among language teachers, only a few general summaries of the evidence are quoted.

MODE OF PRESENTATION[1]

This subject would not require special emphasis except for certain misconceptions that have survived in literature on language methodology. Professor Handschin, in enumerating the principles that have been definitely established states: "If the fourfold learning of language is to be accomplished the first approach should be aural, the second oral."[2] On the other hand, an opinion by Meumann states that "visual presentation has great significance in the teaching of modern languages, and ... the purely auditory or vocal method which is now being recommended is one-sided and unwarranted."[3] The general attitude at present is to assume that the relative value of the modes of presentation (i.e., of sensory modality) varies with circumstances, and the great problem is to discover the effect of these varying circumstances.

A list of the attempts to establish a general superiority of auditory or of visual presentation would

---

[1] A review of some of the experiments that fall under this heading is contained in F. O'Brien's "A Qualitative Investigation of the Effect of Mode of Presentation upon the Process of Learning," *Am. Jour. Psy.*, 1921, p. 249. Other reviews are contained in G. M. Whipple's *Manual of Mental and Psychical Tests*, Vol. II (1915), and in the report of the Canadian Committee of the Modern Language Study.

[2] *Methods of Teaching Modern Foreign Languages*, p. 45.

[3] *The Psychology of Learning*, p. 157.

reveal extraordinary discrepancies in the results. On this point only a few summaries will be quoted.

Whipple, reviewing the status of the question up to 1915, states:

... a complete isolation of the different modalities cannot be accomplished by different forms of presentation: e.g., auditory-minded subjects may actually retain and reproduce impressions presented to the eye in auditory, or mainly auditory, terms. ... These facts account for much of the divergence and seeming contradiction in the results of various investigators with regard to the relative advantage of addressing stimuli to different senses.

With regard to the relative advantages of auditory over visual presentation, Kemsies found presentation by ear better for Latin words and for nonsense syllables; Von Sybel found auditory presentation better than visual for both auditory and visual types of subjects; Henmon found as his most striking result a marked superiority of auditory over visual presentation for all his subjects and for all forms of material. Hawkins reported that ten nouns heard are recalled better than ten nouns successively seen in the case of younger subjects, but that the reverse holds true for above 15 years. Pohlmann's extensive experiments, which are criticized by Henmon because of being conducted by the group method, show that auditory presentation is better for meaningful material (words), while the reverse is true with non-significant material (digits and nonsense syllables). On the other hand the superiority of visual over auditory presentation appears in the tables and charts of Smedley and in Chambers' results for 7th and 8th grade pupils.

With regard to the advantage of combined appeal to eye and ear, or to eye, ear and motor memory (articulation or writing) there are similar discrepancies. . . .[4]

The status of the controversy in 1928 is resumed in the report of the Canadian Committee:

(a) Much reading and much thinking may go on without any discoverable imagery.

(b) The sense department in which a subject matter is presented is not of necessity the one in which it is recalled.

(c) The type of imagery used (if any) in recall of words, objects, etc., depends to a considerable degree on the immediate environment, and largely on previous training.

(d) The important neurological process in learning is not the receptor, but rather the cortex. It probably makes little difference (except that due to previous training) by what endorgan the stimulus is received, (provided it is 'adequate'). . . .

If this interpretation is correct, it makes but little difference whether the presentation is auditory or visual or one requiring articulation so long as two criteria are met: (1) that it stimulates the student to active effort; for learning goes on only when the subject is active; it is never a process of 'passive absorption'; (2) that it provides practice in doing the type of thing the student

[4] *Manual of Mental and Physical Tests*, II, 189.

wants to know. If it is desired to form an oral speech habit, articulation must be an important part of the method; if the emphasis is on silent reading, the student must be practised in rapid visual recognition, since this is the function he wishes to use. As Judd points out, there is no one best method, and this is especially so in connection with the sense department to which presentation is made.[5]

Symonds points out in a recent article that learning depends more than is usually realized upon "clearness and vividness of stimuli."[6] The important point seems to be the quality of the presentation rather than the sense department to which the appeal is made.

PART AND WHOLE METHODS OF LEARNING[7]

Ebbinghaus, in an early experiment, formulated the law that difficulty of memorization does not increase in direct proportion to the amount of the material, but that larger groups or greater masses of material require a disproportionately greater number of repetitions. Numerous attempts have been made to confirm this law.

Only a few conclusions will be noted. Meumann states: "We may regard the following results as established: for adults and children, it is more ad-

[5] *Modern Language Instruction in Canada*, I, 54 ff.
[6] "Laws of Learning," *Jour. Ed. Psy.*, 1928, pp. 405-28.
[7] An account of experiments on this topic is contained in H. R. Douglass, "A Summary of the Experimental Data on Certain Phases of Memory," *Ped. Sem.*, 1927, p. 109.

vantageous, and it is psychologically and pedagogically more appropriate to learn every sort of material as a whole than to break it up into parts''; ''... it is not desirable to reduce to a minimum the amount which is to be learned at a sitting, as one must infer from the law of Ebbinghaus, but the task assigned for a single period must be as great as the capacity of the learner permits''; ''... the increased retention resulting from the employment of the whole-procedure is great in proportion as the group is large.''[8]

Robinson, writing in 1924, summarizes a later status of the question as follows:

> The issue is plainly in a very unsettled condition. Perhaps the question as stated is too large for a single generalization. . . . Interest, confidence, visible accomplishment and recency are on the side of the part method, while meaning, outlining and permanency are on the side of the whole method.[9]

McGeoch writes in 1928:

> The relative advantages of the two methods is, according to the work of Sawdon, a function of the nature of the material. The whole method is superior for average boys between ten and thirteen, with easy, rhythmic and meaningful poetry, but this advantage disappears with difficult material, disconnected material and lack of rhythm. ... The work of Winch and of Sawdon indicate that the

[8] *Op. cit.*, pp. 49, 278, 241.
[9] ''Memory,'' *Psy. Bull.*, XXI (Oct., 1924), 569-91.

nature of the material and the total time involved are important variables in the part-whole problem. Reed has worked over the data on this problem prior to 1925, and finds the facts less favorable to the whole method than has generally been thought, especially by textbook writers.[10]

The question of whole or part method bears a relation to certain problems of language teaching, e.g., whether to give detailed vocabulary study in small amounts, or to trust to a more gradual absorption through extensive reading. A recent opinion by Hunter is that the results of the experiments on whole *versus* part learning are "too conflicting to justify a conclusion in favor of either."[11]

[10] "Memory," *Psy. Bull.*, XXV (Sept., 1928), 513-49.
[11] "Learning, II. Experimental Studies of Learning," in *The Foundations of Experimental Psychology*, pp. 564-627.

The experiment of Reed, mentioned by McGeoch, is interesting because of his interpretation of previous experiments and his unambiguous results in favor of the part method. Reed explains the matter as follows: " . . . the mind in learning a quantity of material must proceed by steps just as the body does in covering a quantity of space. The extent of that step is fixed just as much as the bodily step, and just as the body falls flat when it tries to take too large a step, so the mind literally falls when it tries, in one act, to comprehend a material that is much beyond its memory span. It simply does not get it, and, in fact, it gets less than if it proceeded by small steps. . . . The significance of this for the economy of learning is evident. It means that the mind can learn only by parts, no matter what the method of reading is. If the whole method is followed, it means that different parts come above the memorial threshold at different times. If the part method is followed, fewer readings will be required to bring the part above this threshold. The optimum learning unit must be adjusted to the learner's memory span." H. B. Reed, "Part and Whole Methods of Learning," *Jour. Ed. Psy.*, XV (1924), 107-15.

INFLUENCE OF ASSOCIATION (CONTEXT)

On the value of associative aids in the memory (or learning) process, there is little conflicting testimony. The following experiments are in essential agreement:

Balban[12] studied association in relation to the rate of learning and of forgetting. The materials used were a series of twenty unrelated word pairs. The observers were instructed to learn one-half logically, and the other half mechanically. The logically learned series gave an average of 33.9 successes in recall, the mechanically learned, 7.9.

Buseman (1911)[13] made group tests with school children, by reading to them pairs of concrete nouns, abstract nouns, adjectives, verbs, and nonsense words. The per cent recalled varied from 80.5 in the case of concrete nouns to 14 per cent in the case of the nonsense words. The proportion of associative aids was found to correspond exactly with the ease of recall of the different classes of words, e.g., 88 per cent in the case of concrete nouns, 54 per cent in the case of nonsense words.

Müller (1911)[14] studied the associative aids used by one subject who had a memory span for seventy-two numbers. He concludes that he is justified in setting up a general law that exceptional memory performances are conditioned by the coöperation of natural aids. He notes that asso-

[12] "Ueber den Unterschied des logischen und mechanischen Gedächtnisses," *Zeit. f. Psychol.*, 1910, pp. 379-400.
[13] "Lernen und Behalten," *Zeit. f. Angew. Psychol.*, 1911, pp. 211-71.
[14] In *Zeit f. Psychol., Erg-Bd.* 5, 1911.

ciation shortens the learning time and increases retention. In some cases, however, the associative helps lead to a reproduction of the aid rather than the associated member.

A summary of previous experiments is contained in the report of an experiment by Reed.[15] Reed in his study used series of word pairs, two English series, one German-English, and one series of nonsense syllable pairs. Twenty-seven adult subjects were used, eighteen of whom reported immediately after each response what they had thought of between the stimulus and the response. The experimenter kept a record of every association.

The difference in the rate of forgetting in relation to the number of associations formed was striking. Of the pairs forgotten quickly, only 39-62 per cent were learned by associative aids, whereas 68-87 per cent of the slowly forgotten pairs had aids. The experimenter concludes that word pairs are quickly learned and slowly forgotten by means of associative aids. The absence of these associates produces slow learning and quick forgetting.

A study of the particular kinds of associations used reveals the fact that nearly all are connected with both words of a pair. Logical associations reduce the rate of learning much more than sensory associations. Of the total errors made, only 6.28 per cent are due to associative aids. In all these cases, the aid was reproduced instead of the associate. There are almost no errors due to logical associations.[16]

[15] "Associative Aids," *Psy. Rev.*, XXV, 128-55.

[16] A conclusion similar to Reed's was reached by Klemm and Olsson who compared mechanical aids with meaningful aids. The logical aids yielded superior retention after intervals up to 476 days. Logical factors were found by Washburne also to favor recall. Quoted by McGeoch, *op. cit.*)

An experiment by Shuh Pan[17] tested the effect of adding various contextual words between the members of a word pair. Fifty-six adult subjects took part in the experiment. The principal conclusions were as follows: (1) The presence of a word context logically related to the response word or to both the response word and the stimulus word facilitates learning. (2) A variable context is not so favorable as one that is constant. (3) Other varieties of context, i.e., unrelated materials, are detrimental.

In all these studies there appears to be little difference of opinion concerning the effect of logical associations. Meumann[18] states that immediate retention appears to be the special effect of association. Bonsfield remarks that "... it may be stated as a broad general principle that no memory can be evoked without the aid of a relevant association link or tag to ecphorize the record. This may be taken as a rule without exception...." He adds that "most trivial matters escape recollection because they have occurred without sufficient attention to forge the association links necessary for recall."[19]

[17] "Influence of Context upon Learning and Recall," *Jour. Exp. Psy.*, vol. 9, 1926, pp. 468-491.

[18] *Op. cit.*, p. 114.

[19] *The Basis of Memory.*

An experiment by R. S. Woodworth, "A Contribution to the Question of Quick Learning and Quick Forgetting," (cited in *Modern Language Instruction in Canada*, I, 325), presents incidental confirmation of the effect of association.

INFLUENCE OF COMPLEXITY AND DISSIMILARITY

The principle involved is that the chances of a fact being recalled are in proportion to the number of connections between it and the rest of our experience. It is generally recognized that complexity and dissimilarity affect the memory through interest and attention. The principal problem is to determine the point at which distraction begins.

Certain phases of the problem have been investigated by Gordon, Kuhlmann and Calkins.[20] The general conclusion of these experimenters is that whatever serves to distinguish a thing from a group makes it better remembered. A greater length, a different color, a more frequent repetition, an unusual position are some of the variations that have been tested.

Peterson[21] found that for immediate recall of a series, variations in size offered a slight advantage, that color variation was of no aid, and variations in the style of print were detrimental. In recall after twenty-four hours, however, the result was quite different. Size was the best variation, color next, while even form variations showed a gain of 19 per cent. In the case of nonsense syllables, the memory is improved by the addition of a few variations, but if the number is increased considerably, distraction enters, and there may be a loss.

[20] A review of these experiments is contained in the report of the Peterson experiment, mentioned below.
[21] "On the Influence of Complexity and Dissimilarity on Memory," *Psy. Rev. Mon.*, Nov., 1909, No. 49.

An experiment by Achilles[22] with color and size variations in lists of nonsense syllables failed to produce any striking results. In this experiment, as in Peterson's, the variations were not used for emphasis, that is, not to give greater value to some elements than to others. In fact, Peterson remarks that "if the variation takes the form of experiencing fewer of one thing than of another, the memory for the few is certainly better than the memory for the many."

McGeoch[23] mentions an experiment by Welch and Burnett in which pictures, colors, and other devices were used to produce vividness in connection with nonsense syllables. The experimenters found that the use of these devices assisted learning.

An experiment by Galli[24] reviewed in *Psychological Abstracts*, 1928, shows the superiority of colored over black figures, of complex over simple figures, and of form over color in producing correct responses.

TRANSFER AND INTERFERENCE

On this vast and difficult problem only a few general conclusions and summaries can be cited. Experimental investigations of the particular question of bilingual interference, are reviewed later (see pp. 135 ff.).

[22] "Experimental Studies in Recall and Recognition," *Arch. of Psy.*, XL (1920), 80.
[23] *Op. cit.*
[24] "Ricerche sui rapporti esistenti tra la complessità dei fenomoni associati et la forza della associazione," *Publ. Univ. Cattol. Sacro Cuore*, Milano, I (1925), 113-64.

LEARNING AND RECALL 55

Gates summarizes the conclusions as follows:

(1) The effect of training in one type of memory or perception or reasoning is usually a marked increase in the specific function trained. (2) There is relatively little improvement in memorizing when the form of learning or the material learned is different, even if only slightly different. (3) There is occasionally complete absence of transfer or negative transfer.[25]

Sandiford states:

(1) The transfer effect of training may be negative, zero or positive. It is usually positive, but the amounts are usually much nearer to zero than to 100 per cent. (2) If the transfer effect is considerable, it is invariably found that the contents (or methods of presentation) of the testing and training materials have many elements in common. (3) There is little ground for the belief that the intellect secures an all-round training from the specific training of any part of it.[26]

Bagley, quoting Thorndike, states:

Improvement in any single mental function, need not improve the ability in functions commonly called by the same name. It may injure it. . . . Improvement in any single mental function rarely brings about equal improvement in any other function, no matter how similar, for the working of every mental function group is conditioned by the nature of the data in each particular case.[27]

[25] *Elementary Psychology*, p. 514.
[26] *Educational Psychology*, p. 293.
[27] *The Educative Process*, p. 231.

Whipple, in a recent critical review of the subject states that,

> it is not only probable, but fairly certain, that some of the most important agencies of transfer are to be found among the higher-level relations, in generalized attitudes, moods, ideals, sets, ways of going about mental operations generally.[28]

The following experimental studies relate particularly to transfer of training in language study.

Starch,[29] in an investigation of the effect of language study, concludes that knowledge of a foreign language increases ability in English grammar, but only slightly the ability to use English correctly. He found some indication, however, that speed of reading is probably increased by language study.

Professor Werner, in an examination of the improvement in English by high school and college students reaches the following conclusion:

> Our net conclusion is (a) that it is difficult to defend the general statement that the study of a modern foreign language will always aid in the development of desirable abilities in English; (b) . . . the study of modern foreign languages materially aids in the development of speed and comprehension in reading, especially with high school pupils; (c) . . . the study of modern foreign lan-

---

[28] "The Transfer of Training," *27th Yrbk. Nat. Soc. Stud. Educ.*, Part II (1928), 179-209.

[29] "Experimental Data on the Value of Studying Foreign Languages," *Sch. Rev.*, XXIII (1915), 697-703, and XXV, 243-48.

guages aids in the development of ability in grammar, especially with high school pupils, but not with college freshmen; (d) ... the study of a modern foreign language interferes with the ability to punctuate correctly and also with the ability to discover faulty sentence structure; (e) ... it is doubtful if the study of a modern foreign language, in general, aids or hinders the development of ability in language and in vocabulary; (f) ... the lower the mental ability of the modern foreign language student, the greater is the chance that he will be interfered with in his attempt to develop desirable abilities in English, and vice versa, that the higher the mental ability of the modern foreign language pupil, the greater is the chance that he will be aided materially in his attempt to develop desirable abilities in English; (g) that it is apparent that if a modern foreign language pupil is expected to develop desirable abilities in English his mental ability should be somewhat above the average.[30]

Rice[31] studied the effect of previous study of one language on learning another. He concluded that a foreign language studied for only one year has little transfer value in the acquisition of a second foreign language, and that, in general, the amount of transfer depends upon the length of study of the first language. Spanish proved to be as valuable as Latin for learning French.

[30] "The Influence of the Study of the Modern Foreign Languages on the Development of Abilities in English," in *Studies in Modern Language Teaching*, pp. 143-44.
[31] In *Studies in Modern Language Teaching*, pp. 435 ff.

An experiment by Woody, Hootkins and Carr[32] studied the effect of French upon English vocabulary. The subjects were divided into three groups, those who had studied beginning French, those who had studied beginning Latin, and those who had not studied a foreign language. The word lists used contained an equal number of English words derived from French and non-derivative words. The results were extraordinary: they showed a certain superiority of the "no language group" over the "beginning French group" and over all the supplementary groups. The report of the experiment contains the following statement:

> The Bureau offers no explanation of the causes underlying the superiority of the pupils studying Latin or of the pupils not studying any languages over the pupils studying French in the acquisition of English vocabulary. . . . A different emphasis in teaching either of the groups might change the nature of the findings. But with the situation as it is, the teachers of French must meet the challenge. They should first decide whether the acquisition of English vocabulary is one of the aims to be stressed in the teaching of French, and if they decide it is, they should devise methods of teaching which will result in a better realization of the aim. They should devise teaching exercises which openly and emphatically stress the derivation of words instead of trusting in the blind hope that somehow or other, in unexplainable ways, the connection between French roots and English derivatives will be made. Furthermore the teachers of French must sooner or later resort to more exact measurement than they have utilized in the past in order that

[32] In *Studies in Modern Language Teaching*, pp. 178 ff. (By permission of the Macmillan Company.)

they may know the nature of the products resulting from their teaching.

In general, the present attitude, while not denying the importance or possibility of transfer, represents a strong reaction against the former excessive claims for the "disciplinary" subjects. Professor Coleman points out in this connection that "a good deal of skepticism ... is what we need now, rather than a too comfortable confidence."[33]

VARIATIONS IN MEMORIAL CAPACITY

Thorndike[34] reports an experiment in learning paired associates in which twenty-two adult subjects took part. The materials consisted of 1,200 German-English word pairs, arranged in study lists of 120 numbered sets of 10 words each. The students studied these lists independently, keeping a record of their time and testing themselves for immediate recall. A final test consisting of 120 words chosen from various study lists, was given a month after the end of all study.

Taking the group of twenty-two individuals as the unit, thirty hours of study, plus eight hours of testing, gave command of 1,030 words for three days, and of 620 for forty-two days. The loss in the interval between three days and forty-two days was only 40 per cent.

The study reveals great individual differences in capacity for learning, and also the fact that the ability of stu-

[33] *The Teaching of Modern Foreign Languages in the United States*, p. 96.
[34] "Memory for Paired Associates," *Psy. Rev.*, 1908, pp. 122-38.

dents in memorizing word-pairs is greatly underestimated. The common inference from Ebbinghaus' figures that half the effect of memorizing is lost in less than an hour and two-thirds in a day, is far from being true in the case of memory for paired associates.

Anderson and Jordan[35] experimenting with seventh-grade pupils, found that after two months one-half of the meanings of Latin words and phrases were remembered. The forgetting curve was similar to that for poetry. The order of the different materials, according to the per cent recalled was (1) identical words, (2) associative words, (3) idioms and phrases, and (4) non-associative words.

REPETITION VERSUS RECALL

The problem is whether continued re-reading is more or less effective in memorizing than reading alternating with attempted recall. On this point, there is almost no contradictory evidence. Witasek,[36] Katzaroff,[37] Gates,[38] and Webb[39] found a clear superiority of recitation over mere reading. Trow[40] in a more recent study reaches a similar con-

[35] "Learning and Retention of Latin Words and Phrases," *Jour. Ed. Psy.*, XIX (1928), 485-96.
[36] "Ueber Lesen und Rezitieren in ihren Beziehungen zum Gedächtnis," *Zeit. f. Psych. u. Phys. d. Sinnes*, 1907, pp. 161-246.
[37] "Le rôle de la récitation comme facteur de la mémorisation," *Arch. de Psychol.*, 1908, pp. 225-58.
[38] "Recitation in Memorizing," *Arch. of Psy.*, 1917, No. 40.
[39] "A Comparison of Two Methods of Studying with Application to Foreign Languages," *Sch. Rev.*, 1921, pp. 58-67.
[40] "Recall vs. Repetition in the Learning of Rote and Meaningful Material," *Am. J. Psy.*, XL (1928), pp. 112-16.

clusion, i.e., that re-presentation without recall is consistently ineffective.

Other studies are those of Mabai and of Jones.[41] Mabai's experiment confirmed the law of Ebbinghaus that each three repetitions in learning caused a saving of one repetition in re-learning. Jones found that an attempted recall immediately following study has a pronounced influence upon the decrement in the curve of forgetting. He compared the effects of such recall with those of an extra impression of the material memorized. Retention tests on lecture material and associated words revealed a superiority of from 35 to 50 per cent where there had been a recall immediately after study.

Worcester[42] concludes that one repetition after one day so strengthens well-learned material that there is no marked decrease in the amount retained during the next day, and a second repetition after two days is sufficient to insure a high degree of retention for at least a week.

INFLUENCE OF ATTITUDE

The influence of attitude has been the subject of a number of investigations, notably those of Swift,[43] Panicelli,[44] Sullivan,[45] Boswell and Foster,[46] and

[41] Quoted from Robinson, *op. cit.*
[42] Quoted from McGeoch, *op. cit.*
[43] "Studies in the Psychology and Physiology of Learning," *Am. J. Psy.*, 1903, pp. 201-51.
[44] "Influenza della cosidetta 'volontà di apprendere' sui processi di apprendimento," *Riv. di psicol.*, 1914, pp. 95-112.
[45] "Attitude and Learning," *Psy. Rev. Mon. Sup.*, 36.
[46] "On Memorizing with the Intention Permanently to Retain," *Amer. Jour. of Psy.*, 1916, pp. 420-24.

Book and Lee,[47] all of which are in essential agreement. A frequent procedure in the experiments is to notify the experimental group of the date of the examination in the material to be learned, and to measure the effect of this knowledge.

Meumann states that "interest ... seems to be a fundamental condition, not only of attention, but of memory as well." He adds that "we may formulate the rule that the consciousness of the task should correspond as closely as possible to the nature of the achievement which we shall subsequently demand."[48]

DISTRIBUTION OF LEARNING

The report of the Canadian Committee of the Modern Foreign Language Study summarizes the findings under this heading as follows:

> Pyle, in a study of the learning of an artificial language by college students found that of four periods, 15, 30, 45, and 60 minutes respectively, the 30 minute period gave the best results. This conclusion is in agreement with all other studies on the matter; it is short intensive study periods that educate. Lyon, using nonsense syllables, prose and poetry; Pyle using an artificial language; Murphy, studying javelin throwing, and Austin, in a study of the learning of sense material, compared the values of concentrating the learning in short periods of time with those resulting from distributing practice in

---

[47] "The Will to Learn," *Ped. Sem.*, XXIX, 305.
[48] *The Psychology of Learning*, pp. 134, 288.

various ways. . . . It is probable (1) that short periods, even a half-hour in length, provided they are intensive, are the most economical for high school and college students, (2) that repetitions more frequent than twice a day do not give the optimum results.[49]

In an experiment by Tsai[50] with paired associates, three successive trials were given to all groups on the first day of learning. Six succeeding trials were distributed within eleven days according to three hypothetical retention curves: negatively accelerated, positively accelerated, and linear. The results favor initial frequency with a gradual increase in the length of the interval between subsequent trials.

Trow[50a] found that massed practice is better than distributed for the retention of rote material over a period of one day, but that it is less effective for retention over longer periods. The experiments by Austin and by Gordon are in essential agreement that for permanent retention distributed learning is more effective.

Robinson[51] in an experiment with numerical material, reaches the following conclusion: the relative merits of distributed and concentrated study of numerical material depend upon (1) the total amount of study considered, (2) the units into which that material is divided, (3) the

[49] *Modern Language Instruction in Canada*, I, 57. Pyle points out, however, that diminished returns for long continued practice need not be considered in all cases prohibitive. (*Jour. Ed. Psy.*, 1914, pp. 247 ff.).

[50] Quoted from McGeoch, *op. cit.*

[50a] *Ibid.*

[51] "Relative Efficiencies of Distributed and Concentrated Study in Memorizing," *Jour. Exp. Psy.*, 1921, 327-43.

stage of forgetting when memorial efficiency is tested, and (4) the criterion of efficiency employed, e.g., the amount, the accuracy, or the time of recall.

Ruch,[52] in a more recent article, reviews the literature on the subject, and concludes that because of the instability of the margin of superiority, the value of massing or of distributing learning must be carefully qualified.

REPETITION, DRILL

Calkins[53] in an early experiment points out that frequency (repetition) is "the most constant condition of suggestibility." The general opinion is that "there is no alternative to drill, if it is desired to fixate a form of behaviour, or to memorize for permanent retention a body of material."[54]

Certain opinions on this point may be quoted. Meumann states: ". . . in all learning which is to leave lasting traces upon consciousness, the mechanical element of sheer repetition must play a part."[55] Swift, in reference to the discouraging plateaus of learning, states,

> . . . while plateaus are evidently a distinctive feature of the learning process, it is no less certain that they are unnecessarily increased in number and depressingly prolonged by the rapidity and looseness with which previous

[52] "Factors Influencing the Relative Economy of Massed and Distributed Practice in Learning," *Psy. Rev.*, 1928, 19-45.
[53] "Association," *Psy. Rev. Mon. Sup.*, 1896, Vol. I, No. 2.
[54] *Modern Language Instruction in Canada*, I, 69.
[55] *Psychology of Learning*, p. 308.

work has been gone over. The shakiness of the foundation work is the cause not only of many of the plateaus, but also of the failure of studies to take such a hold of pupils that work in them ceases to be a grind.[56]

Sandiford likewise states:

The factors favorable to the initial formation of habits are also conducive to their permanency. Repetition keeps the associations alive, while disuse leads to their impairment. This is the well-known factor of use or frequency. ... It is from this principle of use that drill in the schoolroom receives its sanction.[57]

Bagley sums up the matter as follows:

Drill, repetition and discipline are the important words in the pedagogy of habit; but the principle that is perhaps most frequently neglected is this: processes that are to be made habitual must first be focalized. Not only this, but a process is automatized the more effectively the more strenuously it is focalized in its initial stages. The law of habit building might, then, be summed up in the following formula: Focalization, plus drill in attention.[58]

There is little conflicting opinion concerning the necessity and importance of drill, but, as Thorndike points out, a decision as to what particular points are to be drilled in or over-learned often involves a very vital question.[59]

[56] *The Mind in the Making*, p. 210.
[57] *Educational Psychology*, p. 238.
[58] *The Educative Process*, p. 122.
[59] *The Psychology of Arithmetic*, pp. 83 ff.

ORGANIZATION OF MATERIAL

Guilford[60] has reported an experiment to determine the effectiveness of a high degree of formal character in a series to be memorized, i.e. of a more or less obvious plan in the grouping of the material to be learned. This experimenter found that a highly unitary form in a series of numbers, even though unfamiliar, greatly facilitates learning, and that the failure of form to emerge, when one of a certain kind is expected, interferes with memorizing.

In an experiment by Laird, Remmers and Peterson[61] the materials consisted of Anglo-Saxon words and their English equivalents, pairs of 3 place numbers and their sums, obscure historical events and their dates. In an organized presentation, material of the same kind was grouped together. In unorganized presentations, these various materials were mixed. Tests for recall were also organized or unorganized according to a similar plan. The best results were secured when both impression and recall were organized. When recall was unorganized, it did not appear to make much difference whether the impression was organized or not.

Washburne,[62] using a large number of subjects, compared various organizations of material. He found the paragraph least favorable for the recall of quantitative

---

[60] "The Rôle of Form in Learning," *Jour. Exp. Psy.*, X (1927), 415-23.

[61] "An Experimental Study of the Influences of Organization of Material for Memorizing Upon its Retention," *J. Exp. Psy.*, 1923, 68-91.

[62] "An Experimental Study of Various Methods of Presenting Quantitative Materials," *J. Ed. Psy.*, 1927, 361-76, 465-476.

data, whether general or specific. The statistical table is the form most favorable to the recall of specific amounts.

Two important experiments in the language field may be considered as relating to organization, although not specifically included by the experimenters under this heading.

Young,[63] collaborating first with Vander Beke, and later with Daus, reports an experiment that involved organizing the materials of the language more consciously and for a more precise and definite purpose than is customary in the usual French courses at the University of Iowa. In the experimental class, the approach was from the "French-English" rather than from the "English-French" viewpoint. The students in this class were given organized study of vocabulary on the basis of the Henmon word count, rules for the relations between sound and spelling, idiom lists, and an organized study of French verbs. At the beginning of the experiment in second year French, the experimental class had a percentile score of fifty; the control classes were, in general, of higher standing (in two of these classes, the standing on the same basis was 77). Objective tests after the first and second semesters showed notable gains for the experimental section.

The experiment was repeated with certain variations by Young and Daus[64] in the first year classes. There were six experimental and six control sections. A prognosis test

---

[63] "An Experiment in Second Year French," *M L J*, 1927, pp. 25-31.

[64] "An Experiment in First Year French," *M L J*, 1928, pp. 356-64.

showed a slight superiority in the experimental sections. At the end of the first semester the percentile rank of the experimental sections was 58 as compared with 34 for the control sections.

A very careful and significant experiment by West[65] is reviewed both by the Canadian Committee and by Prof. Coleman. West tested the effect of substituting words of frequent occurrence for rare words in reading texts. This may be considered, from one viewpoint, as an organization of the memory task. The experimental groups showed a remarkably significant gain in reading ability.

EFFECT OF ARTICULATION

Besides the experiments that relate to voci-motor imagery, already noted, a few studies have investigated the effect of articulation in memorizing.

Miss Seibert[66] after a class experiment in French, concludes that studying aloud has a double advantage in securing greater accuracy and more persistent retention. Barlow[67] studying the rôle of articulation in learning nonsense syllables with 327 subjects in classes from the 2d to the 9th grades, found that lists were learned more economically with full than with restricted articulation. Woody[68] likewise found that less time is usually consumed in memorizing

---

[65] *Bilingualism.*

[66] "An Experiment in Learning French Vocabulary," *Jour. Ed. Psy.*, 1927, pp. 294-309.

[67] "The Rôle of Articulation in Memorizing," *Jour. Exp. Psy.*, 1928, XI, 306-12.

[68] "Effectiveness of Oral Versus Silent Reading in the Initial Memorization," *Jour. Ed. Psy.*, XIII (1922), 477-83.

by means of oral reading. Zuccari[69] found that inhibition of articulation was a very severe handicap in the case of the Italian pupils he tested.

EFFECT OF RHYTHM

Although few recent experimental studies of the effect of rhythm have been made, its value is generally recognized.

Adams[70] has tested the effect of various meters, iambic, trochaic, etc. Elkin[71] found that in learning numbers in series, the less rhythm, the more repetitions were required. He obtained the same result in presenting visually a series of nonsense syllables. Meumann[72] states that "alliteration, assonance, rhythm, and meter, the variety and richness of the diction, all of these play a part in memory."

POSITION IN A SERIES

It has long been accepted that the rate of learning of a given item is to some extent conditioned by the place which that item occupies in the series of which it is a part. One of the earliest studies of the effect of position was reported by Binet and Henri[73] in 1894. They found that in a list of words, those given first and last were best retained. This conclusion has been generally confirmed insofar as it relates

[69] "Ricerche sulla importanza dei movimenti articolatori," *R. di Psicol.*, 1915, pp. 187-95.
[70] "A Note on the Effect of Rhythm," *Psy. Rev.*, 1915, pp. 289-98.
[71] "Über den Einfluss des Rhythmus und des Tempos auf den Gedächtnisprozess," *Arch. f. d. Ges. Psychol.*, 1928, 81-92.
[72] *Psychology of Learning*, pp. 263, 292.
[73] "La mémoire des mots," *Année Psychol.*, 1894, 1-23.

to learning experiments as they are usually conducted.[74] Robinson and Brown[75] found that primacy was consistently a stronger factor than finality. A recent study of the effect of position has been made by Jenkins and Dallenbach.[76]

Binet and Henri point out an incidental fact of some interest, namely, that certain words, for no very apparent reason, are remembered easily regardless of the position in which they are placed. This fact suggests the advisability of using artificially constructed words in memory experiments, since they are less likely to introduce unsuspected variables.

ATTENTION

Sandiford mentions that some form of attention is a *sine qua non* of learning, and that learning is invariably facilitated by concentrated attention.[77] Ordahl,[78] in studying the effect of unrelated accompanying material on the learning of nonsense syllables, finds that this material has no influence, and concludes that there is little subconscious learning, that consciousness must be directed on a particular problem. Meumann[79] points out that concentration and wide distribution of attention are mutually exclusive, because wide distribution of attention is accompanied by but slight intensity of concentration upon particular details.

[74] Cf. G. R. Alford, "Position in a Memorized Series," *Jour. Ed. Psy.*, 1911, 458-59.

[75] "Effect of Serial Position," *Am. Jour. Psy.*, 1926, pp. 538-52.

[76] "Effect of Serial Position in Recall," *Am. Jour. Psy.*, 1927, pp. 285-91.

[77] *Educational Psychology*, p. 229.

[78] "Consciousness in Relation to Learning," *Am. Jour. Psy.*, XXII (1911), 158 ff.

[79] *Psychology of Learning*, p. 177.

An extensive experiment to measure the effect of effort (attention) has been made by Smith and McDougall.[80] In the case of one subject, when making a maximum effort, 13 repetitions were necessary to learn a row of nonsense syllables; in the case of another subject, 9 repetitions. When no effort was made, and when reliance was placed only on the formation of mechanical associations by repetition, an average of 89 repetitions were required for one subject, and 100 for the other.

A comparison of performance after some months of practice showed a gradual increase in the number of effortless repetitions required—in the case of one subject from 39 to 165, and, in the other case, from 45 to 204—a result which was dependent upon the increasing success with which a passive attitude was maintained. In tests for retention, the advantage also was in favor of active learning. This careful experiment would seem to dispose definitely of the question of passive or incidental learning.[81]

ORDER OF PRESENTATION

The experiments under this heading which relate specifically to the order of presenting foreign and vernacular words are reviewed in Chapter II. The following experiments relate principally to other paired materials.

---

[80] "Some Experiments in Learning and Retention," *Brit. Jour. Psychol.*, X (1919), 204 ff.

[81] But note that S. M. Fukuya, in his *Experimental Study of Attention from the Standpoint of Psychological Efficiency* found that "in memory effort is without effect for adult subjects, and possibly detrimental for some children." Something is clearly wrong, and it seems most likely that the error is in the Fukuya interpretation.

Winzen[82] endeavored to determine whether it is advantageous to present the familiar member of a pair first or last. He began with experiments in which nonsense syllables and familiar words were associated. In this case, learning was more effective when the word, i.e., the familiar term, came first. In another series of experiments, pairs of syllables were used, in which one member was made more familiar than the other through preliminary readings, or by being read twice instead of once. In five out of five experiments the results showed an advantage in placing the more familiar member first. A final investigation presented the first member of a pair in large red type. Learning was more efficient when the vivid member was placed first.

Roback and Groetzinger[83] using names secured exactly contrary results. Adams,[84] on the other hand, confirms certain of Winzen's findings.

RETROACTIVE AND ASSOCIATIVE INHIBITION

A number of experimental studies have been made both of retroactive and associative inhibition. In respect to retroactive inhibition, McGeoch makes the following statement:

> The problem of the influence upon retroaction of the degree of similarity obtaining between the original and the interpolated activities has been attacked by Robin-

---

[82] "Die Abhängigkeit der paarweisen Assoziation von der Stellung des besser haftenden Gliedes," *Zeit. f. Psychol.*, 1921, 86, 236-52.

[83] "The Applied Psychology of Names," *Jour. of Applied Psychol.*, 1920, 348-60.

[84] "The Effect of Climax and Anticlimax Order of Presentation on Memory," *Jour. of Applied Psychol.*, 1920, 330-38.

son, Skaggs, and Whitely. Skaggs' results corroborate the earlier conclusions of Robinson that, within limits, the more similar are the original learning and the interpolated work, the greater is the retroaction. . . . This general conclusion is supported by the findings of Whitely that the detrimental effect of congruous interpolation is greater than that of non-congruous material.[85]

In the experiments mentioned above, the inhibition caused by interpolated congruous material occurred whether it was introduced prior to recall, prior to learning or immediately after learning. McGeoch points out, however, that a few studies, under different experimental conditions, have revealed either no retroaction or a facilitation effect.

The question of associative inhibition concerns language teaching very directly, since it involves such matters as the effect of the association between a foreign word and one particular meaning on a later association between the word and another meaning.

According to Robinson,[86] the law asserts that when any two elements become associated, it becomes more difficult to form a new association between one of those associated elements and a third. "If a is already connected with b, then it is difficult to connect it with c; b gets in the way." In an experiment by Kline, states and countries were associated with false capitals, counties with false county seats,

---

[85] "Memory," *Psy. Bull.*, XXV, 513-49.
[86] "Memory," *Psy. Bull.*, XXI, 569-91.

books with false authors, and pairs of numbers with false sums. The results show that if a is slightly, but not strongly associated with b, it is easily associated with c. If a is more strongly associated with b, its association with c is to some extent inhibited. But, on the other hand, if a and b are very strongly associated, a may then be easily associated with c.

This conclusion, if confirmed, would imply the need for learning thoroughly the most usual meaning of a foreign word, before attempting to learn the derived meanings. The principle has received some practical confirmation in the experience of postal clerks who do not lose but gain in ability to form readily new associations after long continued practice with former arrangements.

THE EFFECT OF AGE

Thorndike[87] in collaboration with several others has made an extensive study of the effect of age upon the ability to learn. A large number of materials were used, including Esperanto. Nearly all the results show a maximum learning ability at from twenty to twenty-four years, and a gradual decline from then on. Almost anything seems to be learnable up to the age of fifty or later. The ease of learning, in proportion to age, varies considerably with the kind of skill or knowledge involved. The effect of age, moreover, is often compensated for by

[87] *Adult Learning.*

added incentives and knowledge of economical procedures.

Sandiford[88] referring to the work of Thorndike in its unpublished form, mentions that learning ability decreases at the rate of one per cent a year from about the age of thirty on, so that a man in his early forties would possess about 85 per cent of the learning ability he had when at his best.

Certain experiments conducted by the Canadian Committee, but which are qualified as not being entirely conclusive, show that high school pupils learn languages twice as rapidly as pupils in the junior high school, and that college students excel high school pupils in the same ratio.[89] The results of the American Council tests, reported by Professor Coleman, also indicate "that the ratio of two semesters for one used in granting college credit for high school work is fairly well borne out by the test scores through the first four high school semesters, but that from the fourth semester on the high school student appears to progress with greater comparative speed, in knowledge of grammar at least."[90]

SUMMARY

1. Mode of Presentation. No superiority of an appeal to any one type of imagery has been established. Memories of the various types seem to correlate largely in the same individuals. From a

---
[88] *Educational Psychology*, p. 228.
[89] *Modern Language Instruction in Canada*, I, 466.
[90] *The Teaching of Modern Foreign Languages in the United States*, p. 31.

practical viewpoint, the method of presentation will depend largely upon the character of the materials to be presented, and upon considerations of expediency.

2. The controversy concerning part and whole methods of learning has not been definitely settled. Watt[91] suggests learning familiar matter of moderate length as a whole, and learning unfamiliar matter in parts.

3. The advantage of association in the memory process is undisputed and appears to be of the utmost practical importance in learning language material. The extent to which students of a given age form associations spontaneously, and the effect of suggested associations, offer fruitful fields of inquiry.

4. Typographical devices which lend variety to a page, up to a certain point, are an aid in increasing the total retention, apart from their value in distinguishing the important from the unimportant.

5. The capacity of students for learning linguistic material is generally underestimated. This question, however, is bound up with the larger question of the technique of presentation, and securing the proper attitude.

6. The advantage of recall over possible absorption by mere reading is generally established.

[91] *The Economy and Training of Memory*, p. 124.

7. Attitude is vital. But whether the proper attitude is secured by easy work, stories, coddling, or what not, is another matter.

8. Distributed learning appears to be more effective. It is not the extensiveness of the effort that counts, but the intensiveness.

9. "Drill, repetition and discipline are the important words in the pedagogy of habit."[92] The time for drill, however, is not unlimited, and the particular points to be chosen for the drill need careful attention.

10. Organization of the material, or rather, systematic presentation, is an aid to memory.

11. Rhyme, rhythm, assonance and meter are memory aids. Articulation, besides other advantages, may, in some cases, facilitate learning.

12. Attention is a primary and fundamental necessity. In securing attention, typographical variations may help. Also knowledge of the usefulness of the particular materials to be learned.

13. Age increases learning power through the school years, and the decline in power is slow, not rapid.

[92] Bagley, *op. cit.*, p. 122.

PART II
CURRENT PEDAGOGICAL DOCTRINES

CHAPTER IV

SOME CURRENT PEDAGOGICAL DOCTRINES

The views expressed in the extensive literature on language teaching are so multitudinous and diverse that only a sampling of the opinions can be offered. This sampling, however, is fairly indicative of the various schools of thought and of the present confusion. It must be understood that there is almost no experimental evidence on the points involved. Almost the only factual matter is, unfortunately, the existence of the opinions and their divergence. The problem, in reviewing these opinions, is to discover, if possible, how much of the difference in theory is due to different aims, to varying implications of the terms used, and to what extent the generalized opinions are merely reactions to specific abuses which may or may not be inherent in the methods or principles concerned.

A review of the experimental investigations has shown how intangible and impossible of verification the various "methods" are. The viewpoint of the present chapter is that doctrinal generalizations, also, are contingent upon aims, upon the kind of knowledge to be imparted or acquired, upon varied definitions, implications and connotations of terms, and especially upon the particular details to which the general principles may happen to be applied.

The attempt here is not to decide the issues, but to point out the contradictions, and the impossibility of solving infinitely complex and varied problems of detail on the basis of a single formula, or on the plane of theory and rationalization. The recommendation is for a strict definition or understanding of terms, the isolation of each problem, and for experimental investigation.

GRAMMAR

The program of the *Association Phonétique Internationale* states that "grammar should be taught inductively, as a corollary and generalization of facts observed during reading, and a more systematic study of the subject is to be reserved for the end."[1]

Bagster-Collins declares that

> the immediate value of grammar study is to enable the pupil to acquire the foreign language on the formal side systematically and intelligently. Only essential forms and usages should be selected, and these should be taught by constant practice, rather than by drill upon rules.[2]

Breul remarks that "most practical school grammars contain too much grammar."[3] Rippmann considers that "grammar is not an end in itself and

[1] In Michaelis-Passy, *Dictionnaire phonétique de la langue française*, p. 318.
[2] Quoted in *Modern Language Instruction in Canada*, I, 116.
[3] *The Teaching of Modern Foreign Languages*, p. 27.

should be abstracted from examples and practiced by application in suitable exercises."⁴ On the other hand, H. O. C., in the *Educational Times* remarks that

> with syntactical rules, such as those for the use of the subjunctive, purely mechanical methods are rarely effective, or, indeed, available; the different constructions can only be discriminated by the help of reason. Syntactical rules tell us how far the analogy of any particular construction extends.⁵

These opinions could be continued almost indefinitely.⁶

A fundamental difficulty is that the term "grammar" as used by foreign language teachers has no very precise meaning, and it is difficult to know in any given case just what is to be understood by the term. In some cases, it may mean a certain kind of textbook, or the complex whole known as the grammar method. It may mean a separate academic branch of knowledge, or a practical key for learning a foreign language. It may imply at various

---

⁴ Quoted in *Modern Language Instruction in Canada*, I, 105.

⁵ *Educational Times*, 1919, pp. 142-43.

⁶ A curious fact is that as early as 1833, Ticknor warns against the excessive study of grammar, and advises that "grammar should not at the outset be made so prominent as it has generally been made, nor its embarrassing and difficult portions be so regularly gone through and impressed upon the minds of . . . pupils."—*Introductory Discourses and Lectures delivered before the American Institute of Instruction*, Boston, 1833, pp. 25-43. (Quoted in *Studies in Modern Language Teaching*, p. 83.)

moments syntax, accidence, paradigms, or rules. But rules may vary enormously—they may be simple in their statement, or difficult and complex. The term "grammar" may imply the attempt to treat language as a scientific and logical construction. It has one sense in speaking of the grammar of one's own language, and another sense in speaking of the grammar of a foreign tongue. And so on. The dictionary definitions are vague and confusing, e.g., "The *art* of speaking or writing a language correctly; the *science* that treats of the principles that govern the *correct* use of language" (Webster).

The opinions as a whole recommend more or less of something that is not very clearly defined, and exactly how much more or how much less remains a question. If the body of the opinion is considered, however, or rather the two directions the opinions take, the essential point at issue appears to be the value of a conscious organization of the facts of language (words, phrases, idioms, constructions, usages), as opposed to an unorganized presentation, i.e., the learning of linguistic facts *inductively*, as the child does, or as the person who speaks a language without ever having seen a treatise on the subject. From this viewpoint, "grammar" would signify "organization" and "classification" as a possible memory aid. The opinions divide, therefore, on the question of the value of a conscious or artificial organization of linguistic facts.

Few writers on methodology condemn grammar altogether; in spite of violent quarrels and reactions, there has always been, even among the reformers, a qualified tenderness for the subject. That grammar should not be an end, but a means, is one of the most frequent statements met with (cf. Rippmann, above). Sweet notes that if a rule has no exceptions—or none but self-evident and necessary exceptions—it is worth learning, even if it applies to only a few words.[7] Bahlsen remarks that the reformers have looked upon grammar as a useful means, only maintaining that it could not be systematically taught until there was a certain amount of language knowledge to work upon.[8]

The definition of the function of grammar stated above would permit an exact experimental evaluation of a given rule or arrangement, since the criterion of value, namely, economy of effort, is a measurable quantity. It might happen that one rule would prove useful, another useless, that one arrangement of forms might be better than another, or that none at all would be just as effective. In any case, something to be measured would be specified, and a criterion would exist. The effect of this understanding would be to direct attention away from broad generalizations, which may be equally true and false, and toward concrete details that admit of scientific investigation.

[7] *The Practical Study of Languages*, p. 94.
[8] *The Teaching of Modern Languages*, pp. 28-29.

PARADIGMS

The present attitude toward paradigms is generally hostile. The Canadian Committee notes, for instance, that

> paradigms like *aime, aimes, aime, aimons,* etc., have no independent existence in language. The Frenchman knows them only as jèm, tuèm, ilèm, etc. Paradigms should be taught from the beginning in complete sentences or phrases as, *nous aimons nos livres, aime-t-il Jeanne, mon frère ne parle pas français,* etc.[9]

This question is intimately bound up with the question of the language unit and the influence of context, which are discussed later. It may be noted in passing, however, that, as H. O. C. has pointed out, a confusion is possible between a paradigm as a method of presentation of materials, and a paradigm as a form of practice.[10] As a form of practice, the paradigm may be open to obvious objections, but, on the other hand, if the practice is in the form of *j'aime un livre, aime-t-il Jeanne,* etc., the paradigm as a form of presentation could be retained, and the responses would become as perfect as the amount of practice would permit.

It has seemed unnecessary to point out the differences of opinion on this point, in view of the

---

[9] *Modern Language Instruction in Canada*, I, xxxiii. The same examples and same form of transcription appear in Jespersen, *Language*, p. 423, but in an entirely different connection.

[10] *Educational Times*, 1919, pp. 234-36.

number of texts in current use that contain paradigms. The question is complicated by still another source of confusion. In all discussions of *means* that can have no other basis or justification than economy of effort, a fundamental difficulty is involved. For perfectly automatic responses, there are perhaps no very effective labor-saving devices. In order to *speak* rapidly and spontaneously, the disorganized manner of learning of the child may very well be as effective as any other. A distinction must be made between recognition knowledge and speaking knowledge, and, in school, since time is limited, a compromise is often demanded between the absolute quality of the attainment and the quantity. The attitude toward paradigms, as toward other forms of organization, depends, therefore, upon a variable factor, i.e., the quality or character of the attainment desired.[11]

THE LANGUAGE UNIT

The old grammars often made what Sweet called "the arithmetical fallacy," i.e., the attempt to form sentences by combining words according to certain definite rules.[12] The reaction against the idea that

---

[11] Morgan and Oberdeck in a study of the difference between "active" and "passive" vocabulary point out the importance of this distinction. It affects vitally the manner of presenting the material to be learned. *Studies in Modern Language Teaching*, p. 213.

[12] *Op. cit.*, p. 202.

the word is the unit in language explains the insistence of many writers on the sentence-unit. Viëtor held this view, likewise Breul.[13] Sweet mentions that language, except for the purposes of the lexicographer, consists not of words, but of sentences.[14]

Another view, less frequently expressed, is that the phrase is the language unit. Sparkman[15] implies that continuous reading matter is made up of a sequence of rhythmic sense groups, somewhat analogous to the eye-span in silent reading, and urges the use of these groups in learning a language. Hagboldt states that "the unit of speech is the group of words that convey a thought."[16]

Palmer would seem to have disposed definitely of the word as the possible language unit. He lists a few of the hundreds of words that are monologs in one language, polylogs in another, e.g., "hopeless" *(sans espoir)*, "long way," "leave off," "blow up," "hardly ever," "scarcely any," "cherry tree," etc. He cites *quoique* which is one word, and its equivalent *bien que* which is two. *Bonsoir* is "good evening"; *auszugehen* is "to go out," etc.[17] To treat the individual word as the unit would lead certainly to a fundamental misconception of lan-

---

[13] Quoted in *Modern Language Instruction in Canada*, I, 126, 104.
[14] *Op. cit.*, p. 71.
[15] Quoted in *Modern Language Instruction in Canada*, I, 48, 174.
[16] *Ibid.*, p. 182.
[17] *The Scientific Study and Teaching of Languages*, pp. 37 ff.

guage, and to the absurdities usually understood in connection with the grammar-translation methods.

The question remains, however, whether the fundamental unit is really the sentence or not. H. O. C. in the *Educational Times,* in reviewing Kittson's work, points out that "we can't very well say [whether the sentence is the unit] until a really good definition of 'sentence' has been framed." He remarks that

> the definition that 'every sentence must be composed of at least two distinct parts' should be laughed out of existence. We defy anyone to analyse 'An earthquake took place' into the earthquake and its taking place. It is one. It is all predicate. The whole of our logico-grammatical theory ... wants a spring cleaning.[18]

H. O. C. further states that the linguistic unit is any group of sounds that a native speaker would practically never hesitate in the middle of, such as, "What's the good of. ..." Palmer inclines to the same view in pointing out how certain fundamental units that form a typical sentence may admit of substitution.

> If the authentic sentence is, 'I saw two books here yesterday, it is evident that the word "two" may be replaced by any plural numeral adjective, that "I" may be replaced by any noun or pronoun. ... It is more than probable that a process of unconscious substitution is

[18] *Educational Times,* 1919, pp. 234-36.

the one by which children learn languages before even knowing the meaning of the term grammar.'[19]

In the sentence mentioned by Palmer, it would certainly seem unreasonable and unlikely that *I* (or you, or he) *saw three* (or four, or five) *books* (or pens, or what not) *here* (or there) *yesterday* (or a week ago) would form as many separate units as possible sentences indicated. If language had to be learned as sentence units, each sentence ever heard or uttered would need to be learned separately, and there would be no possibility of original speech. It would be impossible to say anything that had not been said before. But that is precisely what every one does continually. A person sees something totally new to his experience, and he says he saw it, on the analogy of saying he saw the commonest object.

The truth seems to be that no single generalization is accurate. The unit may in some cases be a word, in other cases a phrase, or perhaps an entire sentence. From a practical point of view, the unit must be considered in relation to a given foreign tongue. The principle involved is the possibility of substitution and of combination of the units. "I" may be a unit; it may stand alone; it may be a complete sentence, as in answer to the question "Who is there?"—but the French "je" usually is not.

[19] Quoted in *Modern Language Instruction in Canada.* I, 174.

"Cherry" *(cerise)* is a unit, "tree" *(arbre)* is a unit, "cherry tree" *(cerisier)* is likewise a single unit. "To go" is a unit, "to go out" *(sortir, auszugehen)* is another single unit. Even the preposition "in" may, in some cases, be a linguistic unit: it is obviously unnecessary to learn it in all the possible phrases in which it might occur. The same word may be a unit in one sentence, and not in another. "Outside" as an adverb may be a unit; "outside of" another unit. "At," "the," "home," and "of" may, in some cases, all be units. Each unit may be varied separately. But, in relation to the French *chez,* the whole phrase is one unit. "I-am-going" is one unit in relation to French, e.g., I-am-going to-speak, to-write, etc. *(je-vais parler, écrire,* etc.), but in relation to a language that does not have the "am-going" future, the whole phrase might be a single unit (I-am-going-to-write).

In actual practice, the unit is not difficult to determine if a particular foreign language is kept in mind. The principle involved is the possibility of combination somewhat as in the case of the digits in arithmetic. The theoretical nature of language and the absolute unit within a given language may be left to psychologists or philosophers like Wundt. The question here is merely an expedient definition of the unit.

In any case, it would appear that the often repeated dictum that the sentence is the fundamental unit is neither clear nor expedient. It makes no distinction between a really difficult phrase in relation to French like "I *am* to speak" (*je* dois *parler*), and, on the other hand, "I am here" *(je suis ici)*, and yet this difference is fundamental.

The theory that nothing less than a sentence will do, does not seem to have been thought through very carefully. In learning "I like" why must an object be tacked on, and if so, why "the book" for instance, instead of ten thousand other nouns, and if there is any merit in the addition, why not extend the principle and add "I like the large book of the little girl's sister's friend" or some other complication? It is difficult not to conclude that this represents merely another extreme and immoderate reaction against the abuses of the grammar-translation methods.

WORD LISTS

"Disconnected words," as Jespersen remarks, "are but mere stones for bread; one cannot say anything sensible with mere lists of words."[20] Kappert remarks as well that "it is of little value to acquire a vocabulary by learning word-pairs."[21] Sweet observes incidentally that we do not speak in words, but in sentences.[22] These remarks occur so

[20] Quoted in *Modern Language Instruction in Canada*, I, 22.
[21] *Ibid.*, I, 50.
[22] *Op. cit.*, p. 98.

frequently that they appear to have a common source. Yet the very complementary affirmations would have equal value as generalizations. While it is impossible to speak, knowing only words, it is impossible to speak without knowing words, whether they are learned in lists or in any other fashion.

Sallwuerk explains the objection on the ground that words have no constant meaning, and are continually being modified subjectively by the listener and the speaker.[23] But here a distinction must be made. The subjective modifications of such words as "table," "chaise" or "typewriter" are not a very serious consideration, and the fact that some words have many meanings means merely that they are difficult, not that they can be learned more easily by one method than by another. As West points out, the term "square root" means just that and no more.[24]

If the intention is to dissociate foreign words entirely from vernacular equivalents, it is far from being proved that there is any economy in the devices used for that purpose. The picture method is of very limited applicability, and the Schlüter experiments have shown that the process may involve deception, since the learner is likely (in 70 per cent of the cases) to think of the vernacular word anyway. In conveying meanings, there is no general

---

[23] Quoted in *Modern Language Instruction in Canada*, I, 49.
[24] *Bilingualism*, p. 45.

superiority. *Chaise*=chair much more accurately than it equals some picture of a particular chair. In the case of prepositions, adverbs, etc., the most ingenious devices are apt merely to suggest the vernacular word.[25]

It is quite probable that some words or rather units of expression can be presented better in other ways than in lists, but to condemn a priori a method so obvious that it is the first thing thought of—the

---

[25] In this connection, West points out that, "It does not follow ... because we do not require the indirect bond in the end-result, that we should not use the indirect bond in the initial stages. It was, in the early stages of the advocacy of the direct method, maintained that the second language should be learned entirely without the help of the mother-tongue, and that the meanings of the foreign words should be built up by deduction from their contexts in actual use—the method actually followed by an infant in learning its mother tongue. But the growth of language in an infant runs parallel to the process of idea formation. It is inconceivable that in learning a second language we should go through this whole process of generalization and abstraction again. The ideas which we possess are stored under labels of the mother tongue, and in learning a second language we cannot avoid at one stage or another the use of the old labels in order to find the right ideas.

"It is characteristic of the mind that it cuts out unnecessary processes. The law of learning is from 'complex to simple.' Increase of facility and speed ... comes by elimination of ... movements once necessary but now no longer required. ... The indirect bond, once it has served its purpose, tends to drop out of its own accord. ...

"In devising a method for the teaching of reading in a foreign language we need not therefore be overshy of the mother tongue, so long as we avoid unnecessary translation, and lay such emphasis on speed and facility as to encourage the mind of the pupil and to short-circuit the unnecessary path as early as it conveniently can." *Bilingualism*, p. 251.

CURRENT DOCTRINES 95

method of dictionaries—appears rather dogmatic than scientific.

The disparagement of word lists represents undoubtedly a reaction against the grammar methods and is based on a realistic sense of the interference that the mother tongue may, in some cases, cause. There is also behind the criticism the belief in the desirability of making the pupil think in the foreign tongue as quickly and as largely as possible.

Sweet, as is usual with him, qualifies to some extent the radical and partisan attitude. "In dealing with separate words, it is often a great help to the learner to give them in natural groups, such as 'hands and feet,' 'buy and sell,' 'present and future,' etc. The more concrete a word is, the better it will bear isolation."[26]

A fundamental difficulty here has been the confusion concerning the language unit. Unless a word happens to be a unit of expression, there is no more point in presenting it in a word list than an isolated prefix, infix, or letter. The question is not really how to present words, but how to present *units of expression*. It happens that the largest number of these units *are* words, but some are phrases, and others may be sentences. The question of the most economical methods of presenting these units can be settled experimentally. It seems likely that

[26] *Op. cit.*, p. 133.

much of the criticism of lists would disappear if they were based on an understanding of the unit of expression.

THE INFLUENCE OF CONTEXT

The report of the Canadian Committee of the Modern Foreign Language Study contains the following remarks on the influence of context:

> F. M. Hamilton, H. Eng, A. Balban and W. Libby are agreed that learning a vocabulary is much more effective when the words are learned in a context *such as paragraphs or sentences* (Hamilton, Eng) or where they can be associated by the learner with other experiences (Balban). When students were encouraged to think of *associations,* they were able to acquire eight times as many as when words were learned in mechanical fashion. (Italics supplied.)[27]

A curious fact about the experiments mentioned is that none, with the exception of Libby's, has any connection with the problem of presenting foreign words in context.[28] The word "context" is used in two senses: (1) by psychologists, as any environmental factor in learning a series of materials (cf. experiments of S. Pan); and (2) by language teachers, as the procedure of presenting new words in complete sentences or in connected paragraphs. The effect of *association,* which the Canadian Com-

---

[27] *Modern Language Instruction in Canada,* I, 59.
[28] See p. 27, *supra.*

mittee seem to confuse with context in the sense of "paragraphs or sentences," is quite another thing and has been confirmed abundantly,[29] and precisely the associations between word pairs. Binet and Henri as far back as 1894 found that memory for vernacular words presented in the form of a connected story was twenty-five times as great as for mere lists of disconnected vernacular words.[30] There is nothing surprising in that conclusion, since the story itself was a unit: and the experiment was concerned mainly with familiar materials. The experiment of Hamilton mentioned by the Canadian Committee deals also with the perception of familiar material, entirely dissociated from foreign words. The experiment consisted of a passage in English, first in connected form, then with the sentences scrambled, and finally with the individual words and phrases scrambled. The experimenter points out particularly that "the reader need hardly be reminded . . . that in this study the investigation has been almost wholly confined to the purely perceptual aspect of the reading process, in which only the more habitual and automatic phases of word perception are involved."[31] The other experiments are similarly irrelevant, with the exception of that of Libby.

[29] See pp. 50 ff., *supra*.
[30] "La mémoire des mots," *Année Psychologique*, I (1894), 1-23.
[31] F. M. Hamilton, "The Perceptual Factors in Reading," *Arch. of Psy.*, 1907, No. 9.

Libby's experiment has been reviewed. The Canadian Committee itself has pointed out in this connection that "the conclusiveness of the study is questionable because of the failure to control incentives or relative difficulties of the subject matter used."[32] The sentences used contained key words like *treno* which would suggest the phrase, and there is no telling whether the words were recognized rather than the idea expressed.

There is almost no experimental evidence on the point, but like many other postulates that represent a reaction against the abuses of the old grammars, the theory of the advantage of context is repeated over and over. It is perhaps the most constant dictum that can be discovered in recent literature on methodology.[33] Not only is there a recommendation for complete sentences, but also for connected paragraphs.

The question can only be settled experimentally. It should be noted, however, that the context theory involves a curious paradox. The recommendation is usually that the connected material should be *interesting* as well as connected. Whenever this occurs, the attention is necessarily divided between *interest,* or meaning, of the entire passage, and the form of the unit of expression itself. This division

[32] *Modern Language Instruction in Canada,* I, 316.

[33] Cf. as a source, the program of the *Association Phonétique Internationale.*

of attention would conflict with certain sound psychological principles. What attention might be given to the sense would be lost to the form. If the attention should, by chance, bear entirely on the specific meaning of the new element introduced, the sentence itself would be reduced essentially to the character of a word-pair.

Sweet refers, in passing, to this difficulty: "Hurried reading either of text or grammar results in the learner's forgetting half of what he reads, or in his forming vague instead of definite associations with what he does remember."[34] Again (p. 112) "... we must be careful not to confuse interest in the literature with interest in the language. An absorbing interest in what we are reading, speaking or hearing, so far from helping us to remember and observe the phenomena of the language, has the opposite effect. If the reader is 'panting' to arrive at the thrilling dénouement of a sensational novel, he is certainly not in a mood for observing niceties of syntax."

Bagley, in his *Educative Process,* notes:

This neglect [of habit forming] is reflected in certain fallacious practices that have caused an immense waste in the work of the schools. The wide application of the doctrine of 'incidental learning' is a case in point. This doctrine assumed that 'content' and 'form' could be acquired simultaneously; or, to put it in another way, that

[34] *Op. cit.,* p. 236.

form could be acquired incidentally while attention is fixed upon 'thought' or 'content.' This assumption is a direct violation of the law of habit; the child can never become proficient in form without many distinct acts of attention dealing with form alone. It may be that the child will learn to spell without spelling lessons as such; that he will 'absorb' the form of written and printed words while he is reading interesting stories or writing essays and compositions. But if this is ever true, it is because attention has been divided, now being concentrated upon the form, now upon the content, and flitting from one to the other as the exigencies of the task have demanded.

Similarly, the principles of syntax and rhetorical composition may be gained through the reading of literary masterpieces and the hearing of correct forms in conversation; but whenever this miracle occurs, it is because attention has been drawn away from the content—from the thought or meaning of the writer or speaker—and concentrated on the form. . . .

The doctrine of incidental learning may bring results but it is obviously at a certain waste of time and energy. Divided attention means a breaking up of the continuity of consciousness. At each change there is demanded an overcoming of inertia, and this operates in mental work precisely as it operates in physical work.[35]

Even granting the advantage of context as a general principle, much may depend upon the number

[35] Pp. 122 ff. (By permission of the Macmillan Company.)

of unfamiliar terms introduced. Where only a few occur, it is possible that there may be a gain; where many, that the attention will be diffused and dissipated. The doctrine of interest, which is at the bottom of much of the context theory, as has been pointed out, can easily be misapplied. Moreover, the element of time and convenience (the necessity of thumbing a dictionary) must be taken into account. In actual practice, *words in context* may mean *meanings in dictionaries* or vocabularies, which are merely diffuse and inconvenient *word lists*.

The degree of the confusion on this topic becomes evident in view of the number of functions the connected passages recommended may serve, i.e., (1) as a vehicle for presenting new unfamiliar material, (2) for literary purposes, and (3) as an exercise for practice in recall. Unless these functions are kept separate, the present confusion is inevitable. If the experiments of the author presented in the appendix of this book are generally confirmed, the procedure of presenting unfamiliar units in combination will appear as one of the most difficult and wasteful methods that can be devised.

TRANSLATION AND FREE COMPOSITION

Some of Ahn's famous sentences may be mentioned: "The daughter of our gardener's wife is called Jane. We have faithful friends, amicable brothers, and useful books." "As extravagant as is Mr. N., so avaricious is his uncle." Ollendorff stressed the noun: "Have the Russians pepper? They have but little pepper, but a good deal of salt."[36]

These sentences are curious enough; but it should be noted that they at least meet the current recommendation for *complete* sentences. Essentially similar sentences occur in many present-day grammar texts, and, in cases where translation has been abandoned in favor of blanks to fill in, the same kind of materials may occur.

Although the sentences of Ahn and Ollendorff have been frequently ridiculed, the burden of the criticism has been directed against the very idea of translation. In English we say, "The horse is a useful animal," but, "Horses are useful animals." Since the construction is exactly parallel, we should say, logically, "*The* horses are useful animals." The grammar-translation methods endeavored to chart the intricate passage from the idiom of one

[36] Quoted in *Modern Language Instruction in Canada*, I, 22.
The following is a more classical example of an exercise for translation: "The sacred Tiber, the Egyptian obelisks, the temples still dark with the vapor of the sacrifices, the Flavian amphitheatre, which looks like a mangled giant, the columns which describe the customs of the soldiers, the triumphal arches, the space of the Forum, the mausoleums, the majestic ruins of the circuses and of the baths, and all the remains of the Roman splendor, fill the mind with delightful wonder." (Quoted by Bagster-Collins in *Studies in Teaching Modern Languages*, p. 82.)

CURRENT DOCTRINES

language to the idiom of another. The procedure was often word by word. Artificial difficulties due to the native idiom were heaped upon the natural difficulties of the foreign language. The teacher explained the usages (essentially conventional and illogical) by reference to rules, theorems, etc. Sentences for translation became problems for solution, full of traps, ambushes, and treachery. To use a ready comparison, it was like teaching how to swim through rules for the coördination of the muscles, and then throwing the student into ten feet of water. Much of the practice gained was in sinking.

The absurdities of this method became so patent that it would be difficult to find a recent defense of translation in this sense. Thorndike points out that "the catch problem is in disrepute, the wise teacher feeling by a sort of intuition that to wilfully require a pupil to reason to a result sharply contrary to that to which previous habits lead him, is risky."[37] The Canadian Committee, quoting Sweet, point out that the systems of Arnold, Ollendorff, Ahn, Prendergast and others were "based on the fallacy that words, like the nine digits in arithmetic, can be combined into sentences *ad libitum* by the help of general rules."[38] Widgery states that "translation in early classes is unjustifiable";[39] Kirkman points out many

---

[37] *The Psychology of Arithmetic*, p. 21.
[38] *Modern Language Instruction in Canada*, I, 14.
[39] *Ibid.*, p. 93.

amusing absurdities.[40] "Translation is a mistake," says Breul.[41] Purin implies that free translation should be substituted for translation.[42] And so on.

But translation in various forms still survives, and, according to the particular form, obtains support. Thus Sweet remarks that "translation is a most valuable means of testing the accuracy and correcting the mistakes in our unconsciously and mechanically formed associations between our ideas and their expressions in the foreign language." And, "translation from the foreign language is the most obvious way of explaining its meaning."[43] Bagster-Collins summarizes the values of translation: "It is the most obvious and convenient way of explaining the meaning of a text; it is the most efficient test of a pupil's grasp of the lesson; it is an excellent discipline in clear thinking. . . ."[44]

Obviously, translation has so many meanings that all generalizations about it may be equally true or false. It may mean (1) transference from the native tongue to the foreign, (2) from the foreign to the vernacular, (3) a procedure for teaching the units of language in combination, (4) a test for recall, and (5) a difficult literary art.

Apart from the use of translation as a daily or

[40] *The Teaching of Foreign Languages.*
[41] *Teaching of Modern Foreign Languages.*
[42] Quoted in *Modern Language Instruction in Canada*, I, 137.
[43] *Op. cit.*, p. 202.
[44] Quoted in *Modern Language Instruction in Canada*, I, 108.

final check on the student's knowledge, and as a classroom procedure, with which this study is not concerned, the principal controversy involves the use of English exercises in textbooks as opposed to the use of blanks, free composition, and other substitutes. The general tendency is to favor free composition as a pedagogical device, and it is pertinent to inquire whether this recommendation is due to an inherent disadvantage in the use of translation exercises, or to a faulty use that had become established.

The *Association Phonétique Internationale* is categorical in its recommendation of imitation or free composition as a substitute for translation exercises:

> Quand, plus tard, il [le maître] donnera aux élèves des devoirs écrits à faire, ce seront d'abord des reproductions de textes déjà lus et expliqués, puis des récits faits par lui-même de vive voix; ensuite viendront les rédactions libres; les versions et les thèmes seront gardés pour la fin [i.e., translation is reserved until the student is through, or almost through, with his study].[45]

The Canadian Committee recommend that "after the grammatical problem has been explained, instead of having the pupil translate exercises from the printed page, he can be asked to illustrate the new principle in complete sentences, created by himself in imitation of the sentences provided in

---

[45] In Michaelis-Passy, *Dict. phonétique de la langue française.*

the textbook. If necessary, key words can be supplied by the teacher. By this method translation can be avoided...."⁴⁶

These recommendations are more emphatic on the negative side than on the positive side. There is a deep and widespread sense of the futility of the old type of grammar-translation exercises: these are to be avoided; but the suggestions for avoiding them are somewhat in the nature of a *pis aller*.

It is very difficult to get away from the idea of translation in some form. As evidence, one might cite the series of texts that appear continually, most of which show, in some form, the persistence of the idea. It would seem that so deep-seated an error must contain some element of truth. The fact is that translation is the first means that anyone would think of as a test for knowledge and as an exercise in recall. It appeals to common sense and pragmatic tendencies. If you want to find out whether a person understands a foreign phrase, you ask him what it "means." Likewise, for the student, if he knows *chaise, Stuhl,* or *sedia,* it should be no burden to respond to the stimulus "chair." No one knowing the languages in question would sense either difficulty or interference.

Many of the devices used to avoid translation, such as blanks, completion exercises, etc., have, doubtless, a certain utility in some cases. Incident-

⁴⁶ *Modern Language Instruction in Canada,* I, xxxiv.

ally, the same objection could be made against them as is made against paradigms: they are artificial; they have no existence outside of school, and they relate to little in human experience except, perhaps, to puzzles. The problem would seem too simple to require so much ingenuity.

What experiments have been made have not only failed to show clearly the advisability of doing away with the mother tongue, but the very possibility of doing so.[47] Palmer, certainly no partisan of the traditional grammar-translation methods, warns: "Let there be no illusion on this point; the most fervent partisan of the direct method translates, whatever his impressions to the contrary may be."[48]

In respect to free composition, there can be no wholesale objection, of course. For special purposes and in special situations, its utility would hardly be denied. But in the ordinary elementary class, it complicates considerably the teacher's task. The advantage of common assignments, common difficulties, common criteria, and a common interest in classroom explanations, is largely lost. From the student's viewpoint, the indefiniteness of the task may make it irksome. Moreover, "free" composition in a foreign tongue is, practically, a contradiction in terms, and involves some very curious problems. Invariably the student who tries to practice

---

[47] Cf. experiments of Schlüter, p. 30, *supra*.
[48] *Op. cit.*, p. 90.

expression stumbles into errors in direct proportion to his expressiveness and originality. The race for excellence becomes a test as to who can think least and copy most, so that "free" composition becomes in practice slavish copying. If the copying should become absolutely mechanical, verbatim and perfect, the attention required, and, consequently, the amount learned, might approach a theoretical zero. This difficulty has been pointed out by Sweet:

> Next to the imitation of unsuitable models, the greatest snare in composition in a foreign language is originality of style. In a foreign language we must adhere rigidly to our models. That is why original writers are seldom good linguists.[49]

Breul also remarks:

> In almost all schools composition is begun too early, when the children know but little grammar, have met with hardly any idiomatic turns and phrases in their reading and class teaching, and have consequently not yet developed any "Sprachgefühl."[50]

The present writer's opinion would modify the recommendation of the *Association Phonétique* to the effect that both free translation and free composition should be reserved for the end (i.e., in most cases, to another life).

The difficulty can be resolved by admitting Eng-

[49] *Op. cit.*, p. 221.
[50] *Op. cit.*, p. 13.

lish exercises not for translation in the old sense, but merely for *practice in recall.*. The function of English, in this case, is merely to specify the units of expression that the student is to learn and to practice using. But here also a number of difficulties arise that depend on an understanding of what the unit of expression is.

Kirkman, in pointing out the traps and pitfalls of English as a basis for translation into a foreign tongue, refers to a Scotch minister who was supposed to have urged a French audience in these terms, *"Buvez l'eau de vie, mes frères, buvez l'eau de vie!"*[51] The difficulty here is that "water of life" is a unit of expression that must be learned separately, precisely, and by definition because it is not *eau-de-vie* in French. The question will arise at once how the student seeing "water of life," "scarcely any," "to pay for," etc., can know when the individual word is the unit and when it is not. Without that knowledge, the old arithmetical fallacy could hardly be avoided. The solution appears to demand typographical devices to mark the unit. If the phrase "to pay for something" is written *to-pay-for something,* two units are clearly indicated, and it is unlikely that the student would be trapped into writing or saying "payer *pour* quelque chose." The device itself would help to give a language sense, and would permit the most readily

[51] *Teaching of Foreign Languages,* p. 61.

understandable type of drill. It is not true that words, "like the nine digits in arithmetic" can be combined into sentences *ad libitum,* but that is exactly true of units of expression, since they are, by definition, precisely the elements that can be so combined.

If this viewpoint is accepted, language learning becomes greatly simplified. It is reduced to *memorizing* not words, or sentences, but the most frequently occurring units of expression. The problem of the student of methodology or of the textbook writer is to determine relatively, in the case of each kind of material to be memorized, which form of presentation is more economical of effort, i.e., gives the largest return.

This viewpoint differs little from that of Palmer.[52] Kirsten hints at a similar understanding of the problem. After reviewing the character of the sentence he states that "words (it would be necessary to substitute units of expression) will serve ... in a sentence as addition does in mathematics—in endless combination, function being the most important factor, with the corollary that the language method should resemble the teaching of mathematics with which it has a strong psychological relationship."[53]

[52] Cf. footnote, p. 164, *infra.*
[53] Quoted in *Modern Language Instruction in Canada,* I, 157 ff.

THE "ORAL APPROACH"

The question of oral approach is intimately bound up with the aim of the instruction. Certain writers take it for granted that the primary purpose of modern foreign language study is the acquisition of oral skill. When that is the case, no great issue can be involved. The contention, however, that there is a general economy in the aural, then oral approach, and that this advantage has been confirmed experimentally, is entirely without foundation. The Canadian Committee remarks, in this connection, that "on perhaps no problem in learning is the evidence more contradictory."[54]

Two related questions have been the subject of controversy, (1) whether or not a knowledge of the spoken language is the best means to secure a reading knowledge, and (2) whether language study should favor the "living" or the literary language.

On the first point, the division of opinion is sharp. Kittson states categorically that "learning to speak a language is the shortest road to learning to read and write it."[55] Siepmann likewise considers that oral practice is of value in attaining reading knowledge.[56] This opinion appears to be widespread.

---

[54] *Modern Language Instruction in Canada*, I, p. 53. But see also a careful study by Tharp in *Mod. Lang. Jour.*, 1930, 10-26.

[55] *Theory and Practice of Language Teaching* (quoted in *Modern Language Instruction in Canada*, p. 145).

[56] Quoted in *Modern Language Instruction in Canada*, I, 99.

A frequent argument in favor of this view is based on the contention that the various aspects of language, i.e., speech, writing and reading are psychologically inseparable. West objects that this contention "will stand neither the test of fact or of theory."[57] Palmer writes:

> Many persons are able to use the language in one state and not in another. One who has read extensively and written little, may have a passive command of the language little inferior to that of his mother tongue. One who has listened much . . . will have so sharpened his auditive faculties that nothing of importance escapes his comprehension. But neither of these may be able to express his thoughts in the foreign tongue with any degree of accuracy.[58]

The attitude of West is the exact opposite of that of Kittson; it is, namely, that in the initial stages, "learning to read a language is by far the shortest road to learning to speak it and to write it."[59]

Few would contend that a speaking knowledge is the less difficult accomplishment. The ability to recognize materials presented for memorization far exceeds the ability to reproduce them.[60] The conten-

---
[57] *Bilingualism*, p. 119.
[58] *Scientific Study and Teaching of Language*, p. 65.
[59] *Op. cit.*, p. 121.
[60] A study of the difference between "active" and "passive" vocabulary by Morgan and Oberdeck is contained in *Studies in Teaching Modern Languages*, pp. 213-21. Jespersen (*op. cit.*, pp. 43,

tion, then, of Kittson is in the nature of a paradox, and an explanation of the difference of opinion lies probably in different understandings of what really constitutes a "reading" and a "speaking" knowledge.

In respect to the second point, a fundamental principle of the *Association Phonétique Internationale* is that

> ce qu'il faut étudier d'abord dans une langue étrangère, ce n'est pas le langage plus ou moins archaïque de la littérature, mais le langage parlé de tous les jours.

A criticism of this contention is obvious: certainly if the intent is to learn the colloquial spoken language, it is advisable to study it, and vice versa.

Kittson implies the precedence and superior reality of the spoken language. "Speech has been in every case anterior to writing.... Writing is always founded on speech," etc.[61] H. O. C. remarks in connection with what he calls these "philological dogmatisms" that, "in any case, it doesn't affect the real issues of language teaching the tiniest little bit." He points out, moreover, that written symbols are as direct, natural and as real as vocal symbols.[62] The devotion to a mere phrase like "liv-

---

113) and West (*op. cit.*, p. 116), have both pointed out the relative ease of acquiring a recognition knowledge as compared with reproduction knowledge.

[61] *Theory and Practice of Language Teaching*, p. 5.
[62] *Educational Times*, 1919, pp. 234-36.

ing French," insofar as it represents any thought, is probably due to a reaction against sentences like those of Ahn and Ollendorff.

What should be studied depends largely upon individual needs and purposes, and whether the road to reading knowledge is by way of speaking knowledge or not, awaits more precise definitions of these terms, and experimental confirmation.

PHONETICS

The amount of attention the formal study of phonetics should receive depends mainly upon the particular aim. A tendency to stress this subject is evident in the program of the *Association Phonétique* (and in the derivative opinions) which states that the first duty of the teacher is to make the sounds of the foreign language "perfectly familiar" to the pupils, and that phonetic transcriptions should be used exclusively during the first part of the course.

The question of purity of accent, or pronunciation is always subject to the most diverse and absolute convictions. Atkins and Hutton consider over-emphasis on purity of accent "a real danger to the best interests" of foreign language teaching.[63] West points out maliciously that "if the English boy is to be taught to speak French exactly like a

[63] *The Teaching of Modern Foreign Languages in School and University*, p. 9.

Frenchman . . . how much more should the Scotchman and Welshman and an American be taught to speak English 'properly'."⁶⁴

A curious fact, often noted, is that partisans of the reform methods have stressed phonetics in proportion as they have disparaged grammar, and in both cases, the same general method for insuring a practical accomplishment may be involved. H. O. C. in pointing out this contradiction, states: "Whatever can be urged in favor of phonetics, i.e., the formal study of the subject, can be urged *a fortiori* in favor of grammar."⁶⁵ Parker also notes that "certainly from the standpoint of acquiring a practical working pronunciation of a foreign language, the amount of machinery that has been developed for phonetic instruction seems entirely too elaborate."⁶⁶ The same questions arise as in the case of grammar, i.e., whether it is easier to learn individual cases than rules with a multiplicity of exceptions. It is unlikely that any dogmatic generalization has universal validity. The criterion suggested in the case of grammar rules (i.e., measured economy of effort) might apply here as well.

In respect to the use of phonetic alphabets as a pedagogical device, and considered apart from the formal study of pronunciation, there is less difference of opinion. Sweet maintains that the phonetic spelling of words should occur before the romic, since pronunciation cannot be learned [by adults,

---

⁶⁴ *Bilingualism,* p. 123.
⁶⁵ *Educational Times,* 1919, pp. 234-36.
⁶⁶ *Methods of Teaching in High School,* p. 116.

presumably] by imitation.[67] Breul, however, while admitting the use of some form of transcription, believes that the value of the usual phonetic symbols in place of letters is open to question.[68] Atkins and Hutton point out, moreover, that "the untrained teacher can mispronounce the phonetic symbols as easily as the ordinary script. Many teachers seem to regard the script as a panacea for all ills of pronunciation, whereas it is mainly a very useful device for avoiding false associations."[69]

In the actual use of phonetic symbols as a means of transcribing speech, many difficulties occur. A first problem involves the relative importance of representing merely the sounds, or, on the other hand, the rhythm and intonation of the phrase or sentence. West mentions that "the intelligibility of a language is not ultimately and finally dependent upon a correct use of sounds only.... It is impossible to exaggerate the importance of the part played by rhythm in the constitution of the acoustic minimum of a language.... A language robbed of its rhythm soon becomes unintelligible."[70] James, experimenting on the basis of the imperfections in radio transmission, showed that certain English consonants, for example, s, f, and th, were com-

---
[67] *Op. cit.*, p. 50.
[68] *Op. cit.*, p. 22.
[69] Quoted in *Modern Language Instruction in Canada*, I, 153.
[70] *Op. cit.*, p. 130.

pletely indistinguishable to listeners, and yet they understood perfectly what was said to them.[71]

Another difficulty is that, just as in the case of the language unit, no clear decision has been made concerning the unit of articulation. If the word is taken as the unit, the letters d or l may stand alone, and, if oral practice is involved, difficulties in articulation are obvious. In this case, *les amis* would be transcribed [*lez ami*], which is quite false, since there is no such word as [*lez*] (the z belongs with the a). If the breath group or phrase is used as a unit, a variable enters, since the length of the breath group varies with the speed of utterance and with the speaker. Moreover, if phrase groups are written as one word, the symbols become very difficult to read, e.g., [vulevubjɛməldɔne].

A still further difficulty is to determine the kind of speech to transcribe. Should it be the rapid pronunciation of the colloquial speech, or the slow and careful pronunciation? The extremes can be illustrated in French by almost any phrase, for instance, the frequently heard complaint of a certain French boy, "Maman! maman! on me bat!" Should this be transcribed exactly as pronounced, [mã! mã! õmba] or as [mamã! mamã!õ mə ba]?

A fundamental confusion has been due, moreover, to a double purpose of phonetic transcriptions,

[71] *The Intelligibility of Speech* (quoted by West, *op. cit.*, p. 130).

that is, (1) to record scientifically the mere sounds of individual words, as in a dictionary, a work of reference, and (2) as a pedagogical device for teaching pronunciation to, say, English speaking pupils. This distinction is fundamental.

From the above statement of the problem, the following suggestions occur:

1. In an elementary text, the transcriptions should represent the slow, careful speech, rather than the rapid and fluent speech. The omission of feminine e's in French is largely a matter of speed, and they tend to fall naturally as fluency is gained.

2. Since intonation and habits of articulation are of such great importance, the form of the transcription should take account of the particular tendencies that need correction. In the case of English speaking students, a syllable by syllable transcription of French might be advisable.

3. If the slow and careful pronunciation is to be represented in elementary texts, the breath groups should be short, rather than long.

An illustration of a possible practical application of the above principles is as follows: *Les enfants vont à l'école* [le-zā-fã vɔ̃ a-le-kɔl].

PART III
AIMS AND METHODS—A BASIS FOR AN EXPERIMENTAL SCIENCE

CHAPTER V

METHODS AND OBJECTIVES

The question of aims, and, to some extent, of methods, has been treated in great detail in Professor Coleman's report, on the basis of statistical evidence.[1] Aims and methods are considered here mainly in relation to the actual learning (memory) process.

THE DEPENDENCE OF METHOD

As early as 1893 Calvin Thomas wrote:

Quite a large portion of the teaching fraternity are making of method, if not a fetish to worship, at least a hobby to ride, and that to the detriment of the country's highest pedagogical interests. If I can trust my own observation, a person's reverence for what is commonly called 'method' usually varies inversely with his own intellectual breadth.... Let the teacher put to himself the inquiries: What knowledge or capacity is it that I am seeking to impart? and to what end? Let him settle these clearly in his own mind, and then the question, How best to teach? will usually take care of itself. At any rate, it will no longer seem a difficult or bewildering problem.[2]

Palmer points out that,

the most superficial inquiry tends to show that the meth-

---

[1] *The Teaching of Modern Foreign Languages in the United States*, pp. 7-110.
[2] In *Methods of Teaching Modern Foreign Languages*, p. 11.

ods of teaching adopted in any one country are almost as numerous as the teachers themselves; . . . that the divergences of views are not on questions of detail, but are based on totally different conceptions of the whole problem.[3]

This fact was pointed out many years ago by Lodeman:

> The number of possible methods of teaching languages is infinite. The textbooks may be counted by thousands; a bibliography, doubtless incomplete, of French grammars alone published between the years 1500 and 1800 includes six hundred and fifty titles. A large proportion of such works bear the sub-title 'A New Method.'[4]

Awtry, in an article entitled "Too Much Method," says that

> within the last fifteen years the teaching of languages has had encumbrances thrust upon it sufficient in number alone to have choked any other subject in the school curriculum out of existence. . . . It is marvelous how any real teaching is achieved at all.[5]

Many have pointed out that purposes are different and that the same course cannot be pursued in its entirety with every learner. Colbeck, Judd, Kappert, Palmer, and the Canadian Committee, among many others, share the view that "there is no one

---

[3] *The Scientific Study and Teaching of Languages*, p. 20.
[4] In *Methods of Teaching Modern Foreign Languages*, p. 99.
[5] Quoted in *Modern Language Instruction in Canada*, I, 171.

best method." Stated inversely, all methods may be good or bad according to the particular situations to which they are applied.

The country-wide investigation reported by Professor Coleman has failed to reveal a clear superiority of any method. In this connection, Professor Coleman states:

> We may now take it for granted that the choice of a method is inevitably linked with the question of objectives, which, in turn, is linked with everything else: with the length of the course for the majority of the students involved, with the age, the capacity, the background, the interests, the motivation of the students, with the equipment and personal characteristics of the teacher, with the teaching load, and with administrative conditions in general. . . .
>
> The results of test scores, even when supplemented by the testimony of teachers in regard to aims, course content and method . . . have not yielded a sufficiently penetrating analysis of the complex conditions existing in any successful school to enable the committee to name with confidence all the constant elements in an effective modern language course.[6]

The question of "method," in the singular, is relatively unimportant. "Methods," in the plural, for doing some particular thing and for some particular purpose can be understood and judged; but,

[6] *The Teaching of Modern Foreign Languages in the United States*, pp. 234, 268.

as has been pointed out, the attempt to evaluate "method" as a theory depends upon a number of variables and upon other theories which, in the absence of experimental knowledge, must support each other in the rather thin atmosphere of speculation.

THE MULTIPLICITY OF AIMS

Professor Handschin, in his manual on the methods of teaching modern languages, lists the various values of language study under ten headings, as follows:

1. As an aid to purposive and abstract thinking.
2. To give the power to read.
3. For an understanding of the life, art, institutions, religion, and politics of the foreign country.
4. To give the ability to speak and understand the foreign tongue.
5. To give the ability to write the foreign language.
6. For better comprehension of and power to use English grammar, including syntax.
7. For better comprehension of, and better ability to use English words.
8. As a tool for the prosecution of other studies.
9. For ability to interpret foreign abbreviations, phrases and quotations.
10. "General habits and ideals of greatest value."

In another paragraph the author mentions "good will to men," "ideals of social behavior, honor, justice, courage, etc.," and "moral aspects."[7]

[7] *Op. cit.*, pp. 3 ff.

METHODS AND OBJECTIVES 125

Obviously the aims may, in some cases, include almost everything. Kirkman, in his very thoughtful book in favor of the reform methods, mentions as objects of the study, literary culture, information, ability to communicate, international good will, and literary discipline.[8] The Canadian Committee remark that "modern language teachers make no pretence at agreement as to the objectives to be attained."[9]

The revised list of objectives presented in Professor Coleman's report makes a division between immediate objectives and ultimate objectives. A similar distinction, frequently made, is between "direct" values and "indirect." Professor Coleman notes that

> there is evidence that the attainment of some of the indirect or ultimate group of objectives is favored in a superior degree by modern language study; in other cases either no evidence is available, or what we have is difficult to interpret with confidence.[10]

The Canadian Committee point out pertinently that "the criterion of subject values is determined in part by aims and functions, but chiefly by the degree in which they are attained."[11]

---

[8] *Teaching of Foreign Languages*, p. 12.
[9] *Modern Language Instruction in Canada*, I, 26.
[10] *The Teaching of Modern Foreign Languages in the United States*, p. 110.
[11] *Modern Language Instruction in Canada*, I, xvii.

At present there is considerable timidity in respect to all dogmatic assurances concerning transfer, upon which many of the indirect values depend. H. O. C. cautions writers to "avoid the question of educative values."[12] What is technically known as transfer depends upon how pupils are taught. Thorndike, for instance, doubts the "habits of absolute accuracy and satisfaction with truth" that results from getting correct answers to problems in arithmetic in only three to nine times out of ten.[13] The attainment of any end depends upon how consciously and directly that aim is kept in mind. If training in verbal accuracy is an end, it is not enough to assume that translation which may, theoretically, demand the quality will, in fact, insure it. The result may be mere practice in making errors, a habit of careless and vicious work, and the establishment of a standard that permits wild approximations toward accuracy. The same criticism would apply to hundreds of other aims. And nothing in scientific literature, or authoritative opinion will warrant the conclusion that in aiming at one attainment, the other aims will necessarily be accomplished incidentally.[14]

The direct values present no less a problem. Inglis comments as follows:

[12] *Educational Times*, 1919, pp. 234-36.
[13] *The Psychology of Arithmetic*, p. 105.
[14] Cf. Bagley, *op. cit.*, p. 123.

That as high as five per cent of the pupils in the public secondary schools should study a foreign language for commercial or vocational purposes would probably be a gross over-estimate.

The direct values are, for some individuals, undoubted and unquestioned, but such values are limited and contingent.[15]

A peculiar situation in the case of American secondary schools, as contrasted with those of Europe, affects the problem of the direct values. Judd states:

It can be safely asserted that in no country of Europe is the secondary school attendance greater than 8 per cent of the population of high school age. Indeed, in most European countries it is as low as 3 per cent or less. . . . There are cities in the United States where the high school attendance reaches as high as 78 per cent of the population of high school age.

It is entirely unlikely that any appreciable part of this group will either travel abroad or have communication of any kind with people of other lands. Furthermore, we are without an aristocracy. Motives must therefore be sought for instruction in foreign languages which are wholly different from those which obtain in Europe.[16]

Concerning the actual attainment of the immediate or primary objectives, upon which the others more or less depend, Professor Coleman states:

[15] *Principles of Secondary Education*, p. 453.
[16] *The Psychology of Secondary Education*, pp. 226, 227.

> The testimony of a number of ... persons and of various professional groups in regard to the usableness of their knowledge of the languages they have studied, makes it evident that modern language courses should yield a higher degree of ability to use the language than is now generally the case.[17]

From the above discussion, it would appear that the practical values are relatively unimportant, and the indirect values somewhat insecure. But, by the same criteria, that is true equally of history, science and nearly every other subject in the curriculum. Two other facts relate very vitally to the problem. They are (1) that any aim may be legitimate in a given situation, and (2) that the attainment of any aim depends upon how consciously and directly that aim is kept in mind.

A great difficulty is the multiplicity of possible and desirable aims, and the impossibility of excluding dogmatically any of them. To include nearly everything in the universe of intellectual and moral values, as in Professor Handschin's statement, is almost equivalent to having no objectives at all. The contrast between the direct and the indirect values involves an estimate of the relative importance of being able to order a dinner in Paris as compared with "good will toward man" or "ideals of highest value." Although these particular objectives repre-

---

[17] *The Teaching of Modern Languages in the United States*, p. 109.

sent extremes, individual opinion takes on various hues according to the distance it goes in one direction or the other. In any group of teachers, it is rare that any two are ever in entire agreement. The great warfare over the direct method was due partly to leadership at the two extremes, the one side stressing the direct values, the other side the indirect.

An opinion offered here is that no program can secure wide acceptance that excludes dogmatically any values. The best that can be hoped for is to establish a *sequence* in these aims, to determine which should come first, whether, for instance, "ideals" (or the cardinal virtues) should precede the pronouns, or the pronouns, the articles.[18] For this, in the early stages of the study at least, an objective criterion exists in the frequency of occurrence of the different materials. By devotion to a fixed task, with singleness of purpose, it is quite possible that the indirect values would accrue. In any case, it is not the function of the teacher of any special subject to *educate:* education must result from an extensive, complex and coöperative effort. But

---

[18] Palmer points out that there are extreme cases in which one aspect alone of the language is required, e.g., the scientist's German reading, or the tourist's French speech; but in most cases the difference is a matter of emphasis or priority. Thus the tourist requires ability to speak in the first instance, but, in a lesser degree, the ability to read also. *The Scientific Study and Teaching of Languages*, p. 57.

it is very likely that the general interests of education would take care of themselves if each teacher accomplished efficiently a particular and definite task.

In this connection, the question of the precedence of recognition knowledge or of reproduction knowledge, or, in other terms, of reading knowledge and speaking knowledge, becomes of fundamental importance. A decision on this point is necessary in order to determine the primary objective, and the decision affects the manner of presenting even the smallest units of the language.

THE EDUCATIONAL VALUE OF SPEAKING KNOWLEDGE

Few writers on language attach great importance to a speaking knowledge as an intellectual attainment. Sweet remarks:

> Originality of mind does not make a good linguist. In fact, a talent for languages does not imply any higher intellectual development of any kind. The truly original mind seizes instinctively on the most efficient means of expression at its command. . . . Such minds avoid learning foreign languages as much as possible. . . . No phenomenal linguist has ever produced any real literature, nor, what is more remarkable, ever made any great contribution to the science of language.[19]

[19] *The Practical Study of Languages*, p. 80.

Again he states:

> Original and intellectually independent nations which have a long civilization behind them, do not take kindly to learning foreign languages. . . . The imitative Russian and the supple Oriental seem to be often better linguists than the more independent European.[20]

West qualifies Macaulay's remark that "no noble work of the imagination was ever composed by any man except in a dialect which he had learned without remembering how . . ." by substituting for "imagination" the terms "emotion" or "artistic fervour."[21]

E. H. Babbitt remarked that "it requires no higher order of intellect, and no more exercise of the judgment to speak French or German than to play the banjo. . . ."[22] Calvin Thomas points out that

> there is a wide-spread impression that the ability to speak a foreign language is in itself an important evidence of culture. It would appear as if this impression ought to correct itself when one sees how very many people there are in the world who can speak two or more languages with some fluency, and who are nevertheless without anything that can properly be called education.
>
> Among the great unschooled public, the ability, real or apparent, to speak a foreign language undoubtedly counts as a great thing. They look upon such ability as

---

[20] *Ibid.*, p. 82.
[21] *Bilingualism*, p. 44.
[22] In *Methods of Teaching Modern Foreign Languages*, p. 138.

the natural and necessary outcome of linguistic study. . . . All over the country multitudes of boys and girls are trying to learn to speak German, and that without reference to any particular use they expect to make of the acquisition, but from the general impression that it's a good thing to do.[23]

West remarks briefly that "if ability to speak foreign languages is education, then waiters are the most highly educated class."[24]

THE ATTAINMENT OF SPEAKING KNOWLEDGE

The possibility of attaining speaking knowledge in the classroom depends, of course, upon varying estimates of just what extent of ability constitutes a "speaking knowledge." Thomas notes:

it is possible by sedulous attention to the subject continued through a considerable period of time, to teach a class to speak German in the classroom with tolerable fluency and correctness. Any one, not an expert, listening to such a class, easily gets the impression that they can really handle the language. . . . But, alas, it is only the classroom dialect that they speak. Their discourse moves in a very narrow range. . . . On the street, in the store, in society, their German 'conversation' leaves them in the lurch at once when they attempt to operate it. And so they take to using their costly acquisition of foreign speech simply for purposes of diversion.[25]

[23] *Ibid.*, p. 25.
[24] *Op. cit.*, p. 118.
[25] In *Methods of Teaching Modern Foreign Languages*, p. 25.

METHODS AND OBJECTIVES

Patterson, writing in 1923, asserts that

> the mastery of a foreign language cannot be accomplished in the school room by any method, however ideal, under the conditions imposed today.[26]

Grandgent explained the situation as follows:

> If the hours are equitably divided, every pupil speaks for three minutes a week, or two hours yearly, or a quarter of a day during his entire public school career. When we reflect that it takes us, with fully an hour's exercise per diem, ten or fifteen years to master our native tongue, we can perhaps estimate the amount of skill that is to be produced by six hours' practice scattered over a term of years.[27]

West, following the same line of thought, states:

> Three oral lessons a week to a class of thirty boys yield six minutes actual speaking practice per boy per week, whereas the infant has all day, and every day; and, protected by his infancy, he is able to indulge in a certain habit, brilliantly effective for the rapid acquisition of a language, yet liable to cause an adult to be placed under restraint,—namely, the habit of repeating aloud and often, almost every remark addressed to him or even made in his presence.
>
> The amount of power of expression which can be created in a school course is almost valueless, and even if full power of expression were attainable, in what proportion

---

[26] Quoted in *Modern Language Instruction in Canada*, I, 170.
[27] In *Methods of Teaching Modern Foreign Languages*, p. 138.

of cases would it prove of actual utility in the after-lives of the children?[28]

These opinions expressed vigorously at the beginning of the direct method agitation, continue to be expressed with equal vigor.

Not only is the attainment of perfect bilingualism difficult in the case of pupils, but it is an extremely rare accomplishment among teachers. In this connection the experience of the Province of Quebec in securing bilingual teachers is not irrelevant. Dr. Parmelee, Secretary to the Department of Public Instruction, is quoted as follows:

> We have had in the province of Quebec as good an opportunity, I think, as anybody has had, of having bilingual English teachers, and our interest in having them has been very great, and we have made sacrifices in our courses of study ... for the purpose of having all teachers who go out reasonably qualified to teach both languages. We have not succeeded; they cannot do it.[29]

Jespersen, in reference to the inhabitants of Luxembourg, writes:

> A native of Luxembourg where it is usual for children to talk both French and German, says that few Luxemburgers talk both languages perfectly. Germans often say to us: 'You speak German remarkably well for a Frenchman,' and French people will say 'They are Germans

[28] *Op. cit.*, pp. 251, 218.
[29] Quoted by West, *op. cit.*, p. 58.

METHODS AND OBJECTIVES

who speak our language excellently.' Nevertheless we never speak either language as fluently as the natives.[30]

West, quoting Atkins and Hutton, states:

The gifted linguist who speaks four or five languages just as well as his mother tongue is . . . a 'mythical personage,' as is also the man who learns to speak French like a Frenchman perhaps in a year or less in spite of the fact that . . . the narrators of the myth know Frenchmen who have lived among us for twenty, thirty, or forty years, and still do not speak English quite like an Englishman.[31]

An expedient definition of "speaking knowledge" doubtless does not imply the degree of knowledge represented by the term bilingualism; but it is not irrelevant to point out the difficulty and infrequency of this attainment.

THE EFFECT OF BILINGUALISM ON MENTAL DEVELOPMENT

A number of important studies have investigated the effect of bilingualism on mental development. The following account of these studies is based, in part, on the report of the Canadian Committee of the Modern Language Study.[32]

An extensive experimental investigation of the effect of bilingualism was made by Saer, Smith and

---
[30] *Language*, p. 148.
[31] *Op. cit.*, pp. 57, 59.
[32] *Modern Language Instruction in Canada*, I, 207 ff.

Hughes in the case of Welsh children.[33] Monoglot English speaking children in the rural districts of Wales showed a considerable and consistent superiority over the bilingual children in the same districts. The results in urban communities did not show the same difference, but the study as a whole presents evidence of the possibility of retardation due to bilingual interference. The authors of the experiment quote from Laurie as follows:

> If it were possible for a child to live in two languages at once equally well, so much the worse. His intellectual and spiritual growth would not thereby be doubled, but halved. Unity of mind and character would have great difficulty in asserting itself in such circumstances.[34]

Jespersen states:

> It is of course an advantage for a child to be familiar with two languages, but without doubt his advantage may be, and generally is, purchased too dear. First of all the child in question hardly learns either of the languages as perfectly as he would have done if he had limited himself to one. It may seem on the surface as if he talked just like a native, but he really does not command the fine points of the language. . . . Secondly, the brain effort required to master two languages instead of one certainly diminishes the child's power of learning other things which might and ought to be learned.[35]

[33] *The Bilingual Problem.*
[34] *Modern Language Instruction in Canada,* I, 213.
[35] *Language,* p. 148.

West, after a study of bilingualism in India, finds that "there is certainly no advantage in being born in a bilingual country, but rather a disadvantage."[36] He qualifies this statement later by saying that "if a child is bilingual in its receptive aspect, but unbilingual in its expressive aspect, bilingualism is not necessarily a handicap." West discounts the disciplinary value of a second language. He maintains with Jespersen and Suchardt that "if a bilingual man has two strings to his bow, both of them are rather slack," and concludes that the foreign language should not be used as the medium of instruction.

The study of West is exhaustive, and emphatic in its conclusions. In the mass of evidence collected, the following statements occur:

> The Headmaster of the Hooghly Branch School gave witness . . . to the fact that the foreign medium 'creates artificialty and constraint' in the classroom. Mr. Schmidt consulted South African teachers, and mentions forty as bearing witness to the increased interest of the pupils when the native medium is used. . . . The Hon'ble Mr. F. J. Monahan . . . considers that the foreign medium 'stunts and retards the intellectual development of a naturally gifted people.' . . . Loram . . . attributes to the foreign medium the phenomenon of saturation, of failure to make further progress after early adolescence. Inability to study intelligently and parrot learning are at-

[36] *Op. cit.*, p. 3.

tributed to the foreign medium by a Committee of teachers, by Schmidt, by Loram, by Skelton. The evidence . . . as to the detailed effects of the foreign medium are thus not unconfirmed by the experience of other countries—Belgium, Canada, South Africa, Wales, the Philippines. The effects noted are: (1) Lack of responsiveness in the class; (2) Lack of interest; (3) Saturation and inability to assimilate; (4) Lack of ability to read and study effectively—parrot learning; (5) Lack of originality; (6) Retardation . . . and premature elimination of boys from the schools.[37]

These remarks refer, of course, to the problem of teaching other subjects than the language itself, but have some bearing on the value of the active use of a foreign tongue. Other statements contained in West's study are as follows:

The forces which give rise to multilingualism are mainly political in their nature, whereas the forces which work in the opposite direction . . . are mainly educational.[38]

West is careful to point out that the disadvantage of bilingualism is inherent only in the *active* use of the language. He reports an experiment showing the loss in teaching civics in a foreign medium, which amounted to 31.3 per cent when the foreign language was used *actively* both in the presentation and responses. When the subject matter is presented in

[37] *Ibid.*, p. 75.
[38] *Ibid.*, p. 13.

METHODS AND OBJECTIVES 139

a foreign text, however, and the language of the classroom is the vernacular, the loss is very slight.[39]

Other studies of bilingualism in Switzerland and elsewhere, have generally confirmed these findings. Epstein, in an extensive study of the subject, concludes that the study of foreign languages for *expression* should be reduced to a minimum.[40] Stern, reviewing Epstein's work, agrees with his conclusion, and warns against premature language training through foreign nurses or in the kindergarten.[41] Lentz, in a study of language interference, also agrees with the above viewpoint.[42]

The attempts of teachers in the United States to develop active bilingualism in their students are generally so ineffective that there is little danger of bilingual interference in the average American school. It is interesting to note, however, that what saves much practical instruction from being positively harmful, is the slight success with which it is attended. In the case of children in bilingual families, however,—often in the families of the teachers themselves—a serious problem is involved.

[39] *Ibid.*, p. 85.
[40] *La pensée et la polyglossie* (quoted in *Modern Language Instruction in Canada*, I, 283).
[41] Quoted in *Modern Language Instruction in Canada*, I, 282-83.
[42] *Zum psychologischen Problem, "Fremdsprachen und Muttersprache," Ztsch. f. Päd. Psych.*, 1901, p. 409.

THE DIRECT METHODS

The following opinions relate to the direct methods only insofar as they have emphasized the practical side of language instruction, and notably ability to speak the foreign tongue. They are not intended to prejudice a priori the question of the relative value of particular procedures that may be found in direct method texts. What is involved is the effect of stressing the spoken language in the public schools.

The Canadian Committee quote Breymann, the editor of the organ of the reform method, as follows:

> The weakness of the reform method is revealed by a consideration of the aim it proposes for modern language learning, namely, mastery of the spoken language. This is not an attainable objective in secondary schools, since the energies of both teacher and pupil are not only taxed but frayed ('aufgerieben'); ... the objective is moreover, not a practical one, since only a small proportion of pupils are in a position to use this mastery of the spoken language in actual life; and finally, this should *never* be considered the main objective in secondary schools.[43]

The last number of the *Neusprachliche Reform-Literatur* contains a final summary of the results of the reform:

> The Reform has fulfilled its mission. It has laid the ghosts of the grammatical method, which made a fetish

[43] *Modern Language Instruction in Canada*, I, 18 ff.

METHODS AND OBJECTIVES

of the study of grammar with excessive attention to translation from and into the foreign language. . . . But what the grammatical method neglected . . . the reform method has pushed to extremes. In making mastery of the spoken language the chief objective, the nature and function of secondary schools was overlooked, because such an objective under normal conditions of mass instruction is only attainable in a modest degree. . . . Average pupils, not to mention the weaker ones, do not justify the demands made by the oral use of the language; they soon weary, are overburdened and revolt.[44]

Kirsten sums up the matter as follows:

The conflict over the reform method is still after thirty-five years undecided. The chief reason for this is that the psychological foundation was at the outset insecure, owing to the exclusive consideration of practical experience only. Even yet no clear-cut method has been evolved that, in the first place, is sound pedagogically, and, in the second place, considers the psychology of language learning. What Walter and other great language teachers accomplished cannot be imitated by less gifted teachers, who form the majority. The result is that teaching by the reform method becomes unsystematic improvisation, and teachers, although convinced of its good qualities, fail in practice, and succumb to a compromise method that leads to general confusion.[45]

Umbach attacks the extreme position of certain direct methodists, with their Sprechübungen based

[44] In *Modern Language Instruction in Canada*, I, 19 ff.
[45] *Ibid.*, pp. 157 ff.

on insignificant trifles, and of value only for those who can expect to go abroad.[46] Other opinions are as follows:

> The schools where we have found the soundest knowledge of French, both spoken and written, are those few where the first year is spent largely on formal grammar and 'sentences,' and where reading is postponed till the following year....
>
> ... those trained exclusively under the direct method have a living interest in the language which makes them very pleasant to deal with as pupils, but are at all times liable to make elementary errors, and eventually are outdistanced by their rivals. (Bain)[47]

Both Pinloche and Sigwalt protest against the imposition of the direct method in all French schools.[48]

On the other hand, much favorable testimony on the effect of oral practice is contained in Professor Coleman's report. He quotes Professor O'Shea as follows:

> ... a large percentage of our correspondents has felt a need for foreign languages for purposes of correspondence, of conversation, of travel and of research. Conversational need looms larger than any other . . .; approximately half of our correspondents in each group ... say that they have been placed in situations where ability to converse in a foreign language would have been of

---

[46] *Ibid.*, p. 140.
[47] Quoted in *Modern Language Instruction in Canada*, I, 156.
[48] *Ibid.*, pp. 105, 109.

service to them. . . . Accepting the testimony of correspondents at face value, it is apparent that if foreign languages can be acquired so that they can be used in everyday life, they will be of service to a larger proportion of those who graduate. . . . About one-half of high school and college graduates, as they run, will need foreign language for conversation, and at least a fourth of them will need it for correspondence. Only about one-third . . . will go through life and have no need . . . for foreign languages in any way.[49]

Professor O'Shea neglects to mention during how many minutes or hours the need for conversational ability lasted, the number of languages needed, and the amount and kind of loss entailed. It is possible that the loss appears mainly in the *amour-propre* account.

A more important consideration is the effect of oral practice on class work generally. On this point, Professor Coleman makes the following qualified statement:

In view of the widespread belief that a considerable amount of oral work is desirable, and because of the fact that in most schools known to the members of the Committee in which the best work is being done this element is prominent, it may be inferred that the oral use of the language in class is certainly an accompaniment of the

[49] *The Teaching of Modern Foreign Languages in the United States*, p. 13. (By permission of the Macmillan Company.)

best teaching now being done, and may be one of the factors that contribute to its success.[50]

He adds, however, that,

> On the other hand, the mere fact that the foreign language is used in the classroom can have no virtue in itself unless other indispensable elements are also present. In a number of poor schools tested by the study the teachers made a strong point of their oral work, and in some good schools—that lay considerable stress on this element, the results in ability to read and to write were not distinguished, perhaps because the insistence on oral work . . . is allowed to absorb too much attention and thus to obscure the reading objective.

In this connection the Calcutta University commission complains

> We have in Calcutta heard teaching of an English class . . . in which we were unable to understand a single word which passed between the teacher and the taught.[51]

READING KNOWLEDGE

The difficulty of maintaining the prior importance of the spoken language has caused reading ability to become more and more the chief professed objective of language study in public schools. The superiority of reading knowledge as an attainment is pointed out by Siepmann, Cerf, Churchman, Bagster-Collins, Colbeck, Sigwalt, Breul, the Canadian Committee, and many others.

[50] *Ibid.*, p. 270. (By permission of the Macmillan Company.)
[51] Quoted by West, *op. cit.*

METHODS AND OBJECTIVES   145

Calvin Thomas expressed the advantage of reading knowledge by saying that the student can perfect this ability "not simply when he has a foreigner to talk with and to bore, but by himself, in the privacy of home, wherever and whenever he can get a book to read."[52] Kirkman, a supporter of the reform method, states:

> What makes it all the more necessary to insist on the supreme value of facility in understanding the written language, is the deplorable neglect it has suffered in a past still recent, owing both to the excessive attention given by what is known as the "old method" to the grammar and also to the paralysing monotony of the classical construe.[53]

Kirkman expresses another interesting viewpoint as follows:

> It is worth noting here that even for communication on industrial, commercial, scientific or scholastic subjects, it is of infinitely more importance to be able to understand the foreign language, written or spoken, than to write or speak it. The essential in explaining a highly technical subject is clearness, and the language in which this can best be achieved is one's own. Much trouble and annoyance would be avoided, were it always held to be a breach of courtesy to write to an educated foreigner in the foreign language. And even in speaking on complex

[52] In *Methods of Teaching Modern Foreign Languages*, p. 28.
[53] *The Teaching of Foreign Languages*, p. 15.

matters, it is far better that each interlocutor, putting his pride in his pocket, should use his mother tongue.⁵⁴

The Canadian Committee summarizes its conclusions as follows:

> The Committee's researches do not enable them to prescribe a new curriculum, but they are unanimous in their opinion based on observation of present conditions ... that our schools could make more progress under present circumstances by stressing reading ability.⁵⁵

Professor Coleman states likewise that,

> since reading ability is the one objective on which all agree, classroom efforts during the first two years should center primarily on developing the ability to understand the foreign language readily through the eye and through the ear.
>
> Reading ability is both a primary and an ultimate objective. It is essential in order that the other objectives ... may be realized, and in itself is the most useful 'surrender' value of modern language study for after life.⁵⁶

West also emphasizes the greater importance of reading knowledge. He states that

> the need is not English to speak, not English to hear, nor to write, but English to read, in order that they [the

---
⁵⁴ *Ibid.*
⁵⁵ *Modern Language Instruction in Canada*, I, xxii.
⁵⁶ *The Teaching of Modern Foreign Languages in the United States*, p. 170.

students] may enter that vast repertory of knowledge which is contained in the richest of all languages.[57]

It is noteworthy that West's opinions are based on the need for English in India, not for French in New York or Nebraska, where speaking knowledge has even less justification as a school requirement.

Other opinions of West on this important matter are as follows:

> One of the chief criteria of the suitability of a subject for school study, and of the success of any method of teaching it is, 'Will the child go on studying the subject after he leaves school?' Or, 'Can he go on studying it?' Applying this criterion to the present problem ... it is obvious that the aspect of language study which is most amenable to subsequent individual self-improvement is reading.
>
> The reading bond is ... the easiest of the four language bonds. The others, speech, hearing, and writing may be taught later to those who wait for them, are more able to master them, are more likely to need them.[58]

This point seems to be in a fair way of becoming established. In respect to attaining that end, however, a number of serious questions are involved. Partisans of the direct methods may maintain that reading knowledge can best be secured through speaking knowledge, and, even if the general aim

[57] *Op. cit.*, p. 108.
[58] *Ibid.*, pp. 116, 5.

were settled, all the problems of technique remain undecided. Moreover, "reading knowledge" is a very vague term, that may be interpreted variously, and is greatly in need of an objective, rather than subjective, definition.

It has not seemed necessary in the preceding review of aims and methods to consider the grammar-translation method, which, in its old forms, has had little recent support and few defenders. The field is largely clear for a new understanding of the problems.

CHAPTER VI

A SUMMARY OF THE SITUATION

EXPERIMENTAL RESULTS

With the exception of three or four experiments,[1] a beginning has hardly been made in the experimental investigation of language problems. In the field of the psychology of learning, many of the important facts that have been verified have never been seriously doubted.[2] On other points, the results are frequently conflicting, according to the materials used, or the method of the experiment. A review of the experimental investigations suggests the following opinions:

1. Casual or incidental experiments by teachers not trained in laboratory procedures are likely to be of negative value. They involve necessarily a certain amount of deception, and may be used uncritically to give support to theories that were developed logically rather than experimentally. In the case of attempts to prove the superiority of some general plan or "method," the goal-idea of the experimenter usually assures the results desired, or, if that is not the case, the experiment may not reach the stage of publication.

[1] Notably those of Schlüter, Netschajeff, Scholtkowska, and Pohlmann.
[2] For example, influence of attitude, attention, association, and rhythm.

2. Psychologists are primarily concerned with discovering general principles. An enormous difficulty arises, however, in attempting to transfer a general conclusion to a particular situation. For example, the fact may be established that memory for known words in a connected passage is greater than for the same words isolated and out of context. It is more than hazardous to assume, as has been done,[3] that this indicates anything significant concerning the learning of meanings of foreign words, which is a totally different problem. In every case, the application of a general conclusion to a new and particular situation must be verified before any particular validity can be claimed for it.

3. The main reliance must be on controlled laboratory experiment, even if relatively few subjects are used, rather than on mass experimentation. In the latter case, too many variables enter, and the conditions of the experiment are too difficult to control. Mass experiments may show tendencies, but not precise results; and differences of a few per cent mean nothing. They may provide, however, useful statistical data.

4. As a rule, nonsense words, constructed according to a mechanical plan, should be used in language experiments. Actual words, even when unfamiliar, have a certain individuality, and it is

[3] See pp. 96-101, *supra*.

very difficult to be sure that two lists of actual words are precisely equivalent.[4]

5. In view of the present educational organization in the United States, the principal function of the language teacher should be to suggest problems for the educational psychologist to work out. The psychologist, in the strict sense, is concerned with general laws rather than particular applications, and the language teacher usually possesses neither the technique nor the facilities for controlled experimentation.

THE CURRENT DOCTRINES

Most of the current pedagogical doctrines, which are often cited as established facts, are supported by no experimental foundation, and consequently, must be regarded as mere articles of faith.[5]

The terms used in discussions of methodology are often vague and ambiguous. The term "grammar" is undergoing redefinition,[6] and may mean anything from accidence to the "science" or "art" of "correct" speech. Obviously, statements concerning the value, use, or function of something which varies subjectively with the speaker, are meaningless. If grammar, in the sense foreign

[4] Cf. experiment of Binet and Henri, p. 69, *supra*.
[5] Notably the supposed advantage of oral approach, context, and direct association of word and object.
[6] Cf. M. Frey, et H. Guenot, *Manuel de langue et de style français*, 1926.

language teachers use the term, is merely an organization or classification of the materials and constructions of a language as an aid in learning them, it has no important separate existence apart from the materials classified, and the value of the organization must depend on the particular case, i.e., on the amount of material that can be brought under the classification, on the simplicity or complexity of the category or rule, and so on. The value of a particular arrangement can be determined experimentally according to the criterion of economy of effort, a measurable quantity; but generalizations tend to transfer the discussion from particular realities to the atmosphere of abstract, academic and inconclusive speculation.

The doctrine of "inductive" learning, and the momentary prestige of the term, imply nothing necessarily superior.[7] An element of truth—and of confusion—in the doctrine is that attempts to facilitate learning by organization, pedagogical devices, and labor saving means generally, are largely irrelevant when the forming of a *habit* is concerned, i.e.,

[7] The abuse of the term "inductive" is greatly in need of exposure. It is used by many who apparently have little notion of its implications. Its prestige silences argument.

An example of inductive learning is the case of a certain dog that is supposed to have learned to cross a busy boulevard on the green light. His knowledge is doubtless very thorough, and based on deep experience. But most parents would prefer that their children should omit the inductive process.

for automatic responses and perfectly fluent or natural speech. But the procedure requires an enormous amount of time, and, if applied generally to all knowledge, the amount a student could learn would be relatively negligible. This theory would negative the effect of schooling in organized knowledge as contrasted with general experience. In school, as elsewhere, a choice is always imposed between learning minutely a few things, and a bird's-eye view. Certainly a very general survey is all the student ever usually acquires of history, geography, or any other school subject. He might spend his youth learning *all* about the geography of the Amur River basin, or the anatomy of the frog, and likewise in learning to say automatically, with perfect facility, a few practical foreign phrases.

Differences of opinion concerning paradigms, word lists, and translation result largely from confusion on a fundamental point, namely, What is the language unit? The reaction against the *word* as the invariable unit in favor of the *sentence* has merely substituted one obvious misconception for another. "Sentence" is an extremely vague term; a sentence may be a page long, and if it were, in fact, the indivisible unit of learning, the possibility of original speech would be more than doubtful. A criterion for determining the unit of expression in relation to a given foreign language has been suggested.[8] When the term "units of expression" is substituted for "words" and "paradigms" the theoretical objections to lists or tables largely disappear.

The views concerning "context" are based in part on a misinterpretation of certain experiments[9] but mainly on a reaction against translation and word lists. Moreover, a distinction between purposes and results is necessary. While the intent may be to teach meanings of foreign words by their occurrence in context, the meanings may actually be learned in vocabularies or dictionaries, which are merely inconvenient and poorly organized word lists. To start, not with the materials of the language itself, but with an application of the language to thought or literature, may, in some cases, be the negation of orderliness and method. It is like beginning with an application of the multiplication table before the digits are learned.

The unfortunate doctrine of "interest" may justify anything, and adds to the confusion. Interest is variable and subjective at best, and is particularly confusing when interest in *thought* or *literature* is confused with interest in *language*. Interest in the doings of some character may actually conflict with interest in the forms and meanings of words. Learning is seldom incidental.

[8] See pp. 87-92, *supra*.
[9] See pp. 96-101, *supra*.

SUMMARY 155

The term "translation," like "grammar," has several implications. English exercises may imply solving word puzzles by reference to rules—but not necessarily. English may be used in *exercises for recall,* and merely to specify the units of expression that are to be recalled and practiced. The theory that a person knowing one language can save time in all cases by associating directly the foreign symbols with objects, movements and thought complexes has not been established experimentally. On the other hand, it has been shown that a foreign word, e.g., *zwischen,* when unfamiliar and being learned, instead of suggesting an abstract spatial relationship, is likely (in 70 per cent of the cases) to suggest a vernacular preposition, whatever the form of presentation used.

The advantage of the aural or oral approach depends upon the object in view, and on an optimistic interpretation, in relation to the individual's rational beliefs, of the experimental evidence.

METHODS AND OBJECTIVES

The question of "method" which has given rise to so extensive a controversial literature, is of little practical importance. The method is always contingent upon aims and details. For students in Berlitz schools, for travelers, and so on, the aims are necessarily different from those of the public school. All methods may have their place. The worst method from the viewpoint of economy of effort might be justified conceivably on the basis of mental discipline. Likewise, the qualitative and quantitative factors are frequently in opposition, so that a method economical for immediate retention or recognition knowledge only, may be of little value for automatic response and delayed recall.

"Methods" have begun at the top, not at the bottom. They attempt to discover and apply some formula or key by which a great number of extremely complex and varied problems can be solved. The various mnemonic methods have found the formula in mnemonic aids; the method of "phrase types" in learning by analogy; the grammarians in the principles of speech; Gouin in reproducing the natural childlike procedure, and so on. Pelmanism and Hugo have found other keys. All of these methods are doubtless effective in relation to some aspect of the problem: a complete method might need to include them all. The procedure, however, of finding a principle first, into which concrete details must be fitted, is unscientific, at best. Science demands that general principles should be based on a body of facts established first experimentally.

The professed values of language study include nearly everything in the universe of man. The practical or direct values may be stressed to the point of abuse. A remote rural countryside in Nebraska

SUMMARY 157

or Utah may resound with pupils' attempts to reproduce the uvular "r." A boy who intends to practice medicine in his home town may spend months or years learning to greet a Frenchman, whom he will never see, with phrases of the "living" speech, dear to the practical men.

The indirect values are no less uncertain and insecure. Training designed incidentally for mental discipline may only instill habits of careless work. Nothing in psychological literature warrants the view that reliance can be placed on "incidental" learning.[10] Here, as elsewhere, the gap between intentions and accomplishment is proverbial.

Even the relatively specific aims, such as "reading knowledge" are in urgent need of objective definition.[11] "Reading knowledge" in an absolute sense does not exist. Likewise no one can "speak" or "pronounce" absolutely; the phoneticians themselves are in continual disagreement. A philologist may be unable to read a mathematical treatise. Such terms specify an infinity never attained. The change in favor of reading knowledge marks a notable gain,

---

[10] Cf. Bagley, p. 99, *supra*. Cf. also Coleman, *op. cit.*, p. 235, "Whatever be our objectives, they can be more readily attained if we work directly for them than if we engage in activities that bear less immediately on the end in view." (P. 9), "Except in the case of the three R's we can trace the influence of almost no academic subjects on the lives of numerous individuals."

[11] Coleman states, *op. cit.*, p. 51, "It must further be admitted that no one is as yet prepared to say what score ranges, even on the reading tests, mark the lower limits of ability to read."

but the question of means remains to be decided, and, until there is a precise objective definition of the term, teachers may embark on the sea of reading knowledge as they have on the seas of grammar, pronunciation, and speaking knowledge. Some will go one way and some another, without necessarily precise knowledge of the ultimate port or of the points of call.[12]

On another basic and related question, namely, What to teach, there is no present agreement. In fact, relatively little attention has been devoted to this all-important matter.[13] H. O. C. remarks that

> we shall never develop anything like a standardized and permanent system of language teaching out of our present experimental stage till we have clear ideas on the actual matter to be taught, as distinct from the process of teaching it.[14]

Since no one knows, or can know, all of a language, and since students can learn only a very small fraction, the choice of What words? What con-

---

[12] Bagster-Collins notes: "How best to teach reading still belongs to the unsolved problems in the modern classroom." He adds, incidentally, that "while there is no intention of reverting to the humdrum translation method of a generation ago, there are many today who believe that undue prominence given to oral work . . . cannot be defended if the language situation . . . is squarely faced." In *Studies in Modern Language Teaching*, p. 92.

[13] Note that the first word counts date back only a few years, e.g., Henmon, 1924.

[14] *Educational Times*, 1919, pp. 142-43.

structions? What idioms? becomes a basic and primary matter. The importance of some units of expression in comparison with others can be expressed by a ratio of one to a million or more. An astounding and disturbing fact is that the first word counts date back only a few years, and in that field, the ground has just been broken.

The lack of an understanding concerning what to teach has been amply revealed by Wood.[15] A comparison of sixteen widely used beginning texts in French showed that there were only 134 words common to them all. One text may place the word "grasshopper" before the demonstrative pronouns; one may be concerned largely with gardens or flowers, another with conversation on shipboard.[16]

[15] "A Comparative Study of the Vocabularies of Sixteen French Texts," *Mod. Lang. Jour.*, 1927, pp. 263-89.

[16] Professor Coleman notes: "The choice of the basic vocabulary, of the idiomatic expressions and of the grammatical topics for study and drill in the elementary stages of the modern language course has hitherto been made largely on the basis of tradition, of chance, or of individual judgment, and great diversity prevails. . . .

"An unpublished article by Prof. Rockwood giving the frequency and range of four common phenomena in five French grammars and two reading texts reflects the situation (i.e., the great variability of stress on different grammatical usages). The occurrence of two personal pronoun objects preceding the verb is illustrated in the first grammar 182 times over a range of 200 pages; in the second grammar, there are no occurrences of the construction which is found in Perrichon 26 times, and in l'Abbé Constantin 79 times."—*The Teaching of Modern Foreign Languages in the United States*, pp. 116, 169. See also an article by Blackburne in *M L J*, March, 1930, and Chicago dissertation by Sears, 1930.

Texts which begin with stories or other connected material may abandon all order. If the story is Daudet's "La Chèvre de M. Seguin," the student may learn as a part of his basic vocabulary *houpelande, barbiche de sous-officier, cornes zébrées, cytise,* and *buis,* which may not be seen again in a lifetime of reading.

To summarize:

1. There is no present agreement universalized in practice as to what to teach.

2. There is no agreement and little scientific information as how best to teach any details of the subject.

3. A determination of these points has been infinitely complicated by dozens of different aims. The direct values are, in the public schools, relatively unimportant; the indirect values are uncertain of attainment, and not necessarily dependent upon the subject matter itself.

4. A scientific foundation for language pedagogy has been impossible because, as the Canadian Committee point out, "the psychologist . . . is unable to obtain from the literature on the subject any assurance as to the specific functions which language teachers wish to analyse, train or measure."[17]

[17] *Modern Language Instruction in Canada,* I, 26.

CHAPTER VII

A SUGGESTED BASIS FOR A SCIENCE OF LANGUAGE TEACHING

The preceding study has merely confirmed the conclusion of the Canadian Committee, namely that no basis for a scientific investigation of language teaching exists. There is little agreement concerning aims, and less concerning methods. Variations in purposes or estimates of values furnish numberless subjective viewpoints. The terms used in the discussions are ambiguous. The question arises inevitably, By what means can any agreement be hoped for, or a foundation laid?

A first point seems obvious: there can be no agreement that excludes any ultimate aims or values. The way out does not lie in the choice of a philosophy or an aspiration, but in finding a minimum aim that all might accept. The first postulate of the proposed program attempts to define in small but objective terms the subject matter to be taught.

1. The beginning language text or method should present units of expression (not words or sentences, necessarily) in the approximate order of their importance, as measured by frequency of occurrence.

This recommendation appears obvious, but is far-reaching in effect. Few language texts conform to this requirement. The studies of Wood and others (see page 159) show how far astray many writers may go. If this recommendation were generally adopted, the choice of particular materials to teach or learn would no longer depend upon chance, upon the caprice of a story, or upon subjective judgment. The plan provides for the greatest surrender value at any point in the course, even for the first weeks of study. Moreover, it would unify the work being done in different institutions. A student who had studied for a certain period could be presupposed to have learned certain definite facts. No such assurance at present exists, since the present waste is large in amount and different in character.[1]

The second point concerns the technique of presentation. Here the attempt is merely to suggest a basis for experimentation, since generalizations, in view of the complexity of the materials, must be insecure.

> 2. The value of a particular method of presentation depends upon the relative economy of effort it insures which can be determined experimentally in the case of each kind of material.

A corollary is that recognition (reading) knowledge should precede reproduction (speaking) knowledge,

---

[1] West's viewpoint is similar: "... in a First book introducing 200 new words, those 200 words should ideally be the 200 commonest words in English. The nearer they approach to that ideal the better, and any word introduced from outside those 200 which can be replaced by a word of a frequency nearer to that of the 200 should count against the author."—*Bilingualism*, p. 272.

the latter to be attained as the more important material comes up for renewed attention in its natural recurrence.

The above postulates define what to teach, and offer a criterion for determining how to teach. They dispose of the vexed question of "reading knowledge" versus "speaking knowledge": both of these become contingent: the degree of their attainment will depend upon the length and amount of study. Above all, the recommendations involve *measurable* quantities, and offer a basis for an objective science of language psychology.

The question of indirect values does not need to complicate the issue. In cases where "mental discipline," "love for France," or "ideals" must be conscious and primary objectives, the study of language may be postponed in their favor. But insofar as these values are incidental, they depend upon such variables as the efficiency, character, intelligence, and culture of the teacher, on the character and age of the pupils, their previous training, and so on—that is, on a situation, or on an art or an administration, and not on a program.[2]

[2] Two statements of West relate directly to this point: ". . . the discipline of a subject depends on the teacher, and discipline is found in all subjects, and in the whole process of living." Again, "The work of all educational reformers has been to reëmphasize the limitation of the teacher by the nature of the taught."

In respect to the fallacy of indirect gains and the need for precise objectives, West notes: "The fallacy is seen best in regard to adult

The suggested program, by seeking a small common ground of agreement, disposes of general theories and methods that have furnished a battle ground for much controversy and inconclusive speculation in the past. These theories have enlisted enthusiasm, partisanship, and *amour-propre*, have divided language teachers into hostile groups, and have made even the beginning of a scientific approach to language problems difficult. This program excludes no method, and no ultimate aspiration. It provides a basis for dispassionate investigation of the facts, without motives to confirm the convictions of an ardent faith. It directs attention toward concrete details and immediate realities.

The task of the language teacher, as distinguished from the teacher of literature, art, or ethics, is greatly simplified. Learning a language becomes essentially a memory problem: it is the learning for recognition or recall of a fixed list of units of expression.[3] This task is as precise as learning the

education: a carpenter finds difficulty in his work through lack of skill in calculation: he goes to the schoolmaster and explains his trouble. 'You need,' says the schoolmaster, 'a course in elementary mathematics.' He classifies the need into one of his ready-made 'lots' and serves out a block of experience which includes L. C. M., Troy weight, Discount and a number of other items . . . entirely unconnected with the specific need.''—*Bilingualism*, pp. 65, 48, 51-52.

[3] ''Learning and memory are merely different aspects of the same thing.''—W. H. Pyle, *op. cit.*, p. 144. Palmer points out that ''learning by heart is the basis of all linguistic study, for every sentence ever heard or written by anybody has either been learnt by

multiplication table, and might be accomplished with equal efficiency. The viewpoint implied excludes, on the one hand, the illusion that language can be learned as a kind of science, and, on the other hand, the negation of orderliness and method that was due to a reaction against this illusion. The program distinguishes between immediate duties and the remote desires which justify any digression. Moreover, it defines "reading knowledge" in objective terms, i.e., in terms of a concrete list of units of expression.

heart in its entirety or else has been composed (consciously or unconsciously) from smaller units, each of which must at one time have been learnt by heart."—*Op. cit.*, p. 13.

CHAPTER VIII

CERTAIN PROBLEMS AND IMPLICATIONS

THE UNIT OF EXPRESSION

This topic has been discussed in connection with the current doctrines. It is of such vital importance, however, that it requires a more detailed treatment.

Palmer has pointed out the extraordinary inconsistencies in words as units, e.g., matchbox, but not "letterbox"; teapot, but not "coffeepot"; quoique, but not "bienque"; puisque, but not "parceque"; teaspoon, but not "soupspoon," etc. He lists the units that must be learned by heart under twelve headings, as follows (the grouping supplied):

I. (1) Monologs which constitute entities undecomposable into significative parts, such as *go, good, with, children, le, bon, ici, faire, lui,* etc. (2) Monologs that can be decomposed into ultimate units only by the aid of historical etymology: Ex., *perhaps, Wednesday, forget, maintenant, toujours, bonheur,* etc. (3) Monologs not generally regarded by the natives themselves as compounds, more especially when the meaning of the word does not represent the sum of the meanings of its component parts. Ex., *waistcoat, forehead, something, chou-fleur, quelqu'un, lorsque,* etc. (4) Derived monologs or those representing compounds the elements of which can only be ascertained by reference

PROBLEMS AND IMPLICATIONS 167

to the ancestral or some other foreign language. Ex., *imprimer, entrer, bibliothèque, téléphone,* etc.

II. (1) Polylogs that do not represent the sum of their component parts. Ex., *how much, last night, all right, pomme de terre, bien que, quand même,* etc. (2) Polylogs of which the individual parts are likely to be misplaced or confused with others. Ex., *la fenêtre, le mur, du pain, finir de, suis venu, ought to, had better, would rather,* etc. (3) Polylogs composed of elements rarely used in any other context. Ex., *je suis, il faut, rez-de-chaussée, au fur et à mesure, to and fro,* etc. (4) Polylogs the natural equivalents of native monologs. Ex., *en haut, jusqu'à ce que, vouloir dire, coup d'oeil, go in, come back, get up,* etc.

III. (1) Sentences not to be composed by any laws of reasoning or analogy. Ex., *je n'y puis rien; il n'y a pas de quoi; ça m'est égal; how do you do? what's the matter?* etc. (2) Sentences that serve as illustrations of important lexicological laws. Ex., *je ne le lui ai pas donné, personne n'est venu; il faut que je le fasse,* etc. (3) Sentences to enable the student to make use of his knowledge, especially in the case of adults who are contemplating a visit to the foreign country. Ex., *je ne vous comprends pas; je suis anglais; parlez plus lentement, s'il vous plaît,* etc. (4) A certain number of regular sentences to serve in connection with substitution tables.

The material not included as primary units consists of all monologs derived or composed by the normal and regular laws of derivation and composition, of all polylogs not included under the headings II, 1-4, and all the countless sentences not specified.[1]

The criterion suggested in this book would not conflict seriously with Palmer's symmetrical classification, but there are certain differences. Instead of specifying nearly all, it includes all the monologs, depending always upon the particular case. Any word may be a unit, or any phrase, or any sentence. The difficulty always, in either case, is to determine when a given monolog that *might* be a unit *is* one or not. In the phrase *comment allez-vous?* the three words taken separately may each be units, but the sum of the three, in this case, equals one, and if you add *au théâtre* a further variation occurs in the mathematics of the units. Palmer's classification is intended merely to specify what material must be learned by heart, and his definition of the units is bound up, therefore, with an opinion concerning the best means to acquire a knowledge of them. Few would quarrel with his judgment in most of these cases, but a doubt in a few instances might exist. For example, nouns are given with the article which specifies their gender; but if passive learning only is considered, they can be understood without knowing their gender, and the two words do not form necessarily a single unit. Likewise, in such type sentences as *il faut que je le fasse* (class III, 2) there

[1] *The Scientific Study and Teaching of Languages*, pp. 114-16.

is some confusion between the unit itself and a method for teaching the language. No objection might be raised to committing such a phrase to heart as an integral unit, rather than learning the rule for the use of the subjunctive, but these matters should be decided by experimentation and in relation to age, purposes, and other factors that make any generalization concerning the learning process hazardous. The same criticism would apply to the items excluded, such as regular verb forms. *Je danse* is a unit quite as much as *je donne,* although practically it would be learned, in all probability, by analogy with *je donne.* Many hundreds of units may be learned from a single model.

The criterion for determining the unit suggested in this book is entirely relative, and practical in the sense that it can hardly be applied apart from word lists, paradigms, translations of the units, and so on. The difference between possible absolute units such as those mentioned by Palmer, and relative units is illustrated by the following examples: The English monologs *of* and *the,* in relation to the phrase *de la petite fille* (of the little girl), may be considered as separate units, but in *della ragazza* (of-the girl) or *du garçon* (of-the boy) *of* and *the* form a single unit, and, to cite still another example, in relation to Latin *pueri* the whole phrase "of-the-boy" is a unit.

The following passage taken from Act I of *La Poudre aux Yeux* will illustrate the principle more fully. The text was chosen somewhat at random as one that might offer a relatively difficult, idiomatic and individualized form of speech, and as one that might test by a severe trial the possibility of introducing some order in the complicated chaos of words and phrases.

ACT I

Sophie. Alors *(then)* madame *(madam)*, il ne faudra pas de poisson *(no fish will be required)*?

Madame Malingear, assise *(seated)* à droite *(to the right)* du *(of the)* guéridon *(small round table)* et *(and)* travaillant *(working)*. Non *(no)*!. . . . Il a fait du vent *(it has been windy)* toute la semaine *(the whole week)*, il doit être *(it must be)* hors de prix *(very expensive)*. . . . Mais *(but)* tâchez *(try to arrange)* que *(that)* votre *(your)* filet *(tenderloin)* soit *(may be)* advantageux *(advantageous* [as a purchase]*)*.

Sophie. Et *(and)* pour *(as for)* légumes *(vegetables)*? On commence *(we are beginning)* à voir *(to see)* des *(some)* petits pois *(peas)*.

Madame Malingear. Vous savez *(you know)* bien *(well)* que *(that)* les *(the)* primeurs *(early vegetables)* n'ont pas *(haven't)* de *(any)* goût *(taste)* etc.

A simpler passage is as follows (from Renan's *Ma Soeur Henriette*):

Ma *(my)* soeur *(sister)* Henriette (...) naquit *(was born)* à *(at)* Tréguier (...) le 22 juillet *(on the twenty-second of July)* 1811. Sa *(her)* vie *(life)* fut *(was)* de bonne heure *(early)* attristée *(saddened)* et *(and)* remplie

PROBLEMS AND IMPLICATIONS 171

(filled) d' *(with)* austères *(austere)* devoirs *(duties)*. Elle *(she)* ne connut jamais *(never knew)* d' *(any)* autres *(other)* joies *(joys)* que *(except)* celles *(those)* que donne la vertu *(that virtue gives)* et *(and)* les *(the)* affections *(affections)* du *(of the)* coeur *(heart)*.

This form of transcription probably has no utility whatever except to point out what units, if understood separately, would combine into an understanding of the passage. Many of the units represent frequently occurring type phrases which would be learned almost certainly as patterns and not as individuals. In the division, semantic variations are not allowed to complicate the issue. The fact that *que* (relative pronoun) usually has the conventional English equivalent "that" does not mean that it may not have the conventional equivalent "except." It is certainly a great advantage to separate a consideration of the units from semantic difficulties on the one hand and from methods for learning them on the other. Unless this is done there is danger of confusing one difficulty with another.

THE DESIGNATION OF THE UNITS

To discover the absolute or relative units is the first step: how to represent them offers another important problem. The teacher who knows the foreign language may recognize the units at once, but how is the student seeing "to look for" to know that it is, in French, *chercher* and not *chercher pour?*

Or how can he tell when "I am" is not *je suis*, but *je dois* or *j'ai*? There is no attempt here to determine whether word lists, translation or English exercises should be used or not, but if they are used, some method to indicate the units appears necessary. It would probably not be difficult to establish a conventional practice in the use of typographical devices, to indicate units and variations from primary meanings, e.g., to-look-for, *chercher*; it is-necessary, *il faut*, I am to come, je *dois* venir, etc. Bold face might indicate emphatic or disjunctive forms, and abbreviations might be used to indicate conventional variations in moods or tenses. The alternative is translation in the old sense, practice in making errors, puzzles, tricks and so on, or, perhaps, on the other hand, if all translation is banished, a series of illusions equally unfortunate.

As an illustration of a method of designation, the passage from *La Poudre aux Yeux* already quoted is hardly appropriate. If the principle of frequency were applied, by the time the student came to such words as *guéridon* or *tenderloin*, no very artificial studial devices would be necessary. Still the passage may serve by way of hypothetical illustration:

> Sophie. Alors, madame, *il ne faudra pas de poisson?*
> Madame Malingear, assise *à droite* du guéridon et travaillant. Non! *Il a fait du vent · toute la* semaine, *il doit*

être · *hors de prix*. Mais, tâchez que votre filet soit advantageux.

Sophie. Et pour légumes? On commence à voir des *petits pois*.

Madame Malingear. Vous savez bien que les **primeurs** n'ont pas de goût . . . etc.

This typographical device would not be used, in all probability, except for drill exercises, or in material designed to emphasize certain units. The transferring of such a passage from English to French is still more remote from any contemplated reality, but, to keep strictly comparable material, the same excerpt will be used.

Sophie. Then, madam, *no fish will be required?*

Madame Malingear, seated to [the] right-of-the small-round-table, and working. No! *it has been windy · the whole* week, *it must be* expensive. But try-to-arrange that your tenderloin may-be advantageous [as a purchase].

Sophie. And as-for vegetables? We (indef.) are beginning to (à) see some peas.

Madame Malingear. You know well that [the] early-vegetables do not have *any* taste.

The italicizing (or other designation) of words to mark semantic variations would depend, of course, upon what was established as the most frequent or primary meaning. It must be understood, moreover, that the program recommended would exclude (except for possible supplementary purposes) the capricious order of units offered in a connected passage of this kind, which represents, not materials of the language primarily, but rather an application of the language to literature.

In the case of frequency counts, however, such a passage would present a realistic problem. In counting the units, it is obviously unnecessary to list as separate items all the regular variations of forms and pattern phrases, but, on the other hand, semantic variations are important. The following represents a tentative method for counting and listing the materials, using as a basis the two passages quoted:

The items included are: alors, madame, il faut, ne . . . pas, poisson, il ne faudra pas de poisson *(type phrase)*, assise, à droite, de (du, des), guéridon, et, travailler, non, il a fait du vent *(type phrase)*,—and so on.

The combined frequencies, together with the semantic differentiations, would be as follows:

1. General distribution: verb forms, irregular 10, regular, 4; Tenses: Pres. Indic., 4; Past Part., 3; Past Absolute, 3; Pres. Part., 1; Imperative, 1; Pres. Subj., 1.—Cases of inversion, 1.
2. Items: le (la les, l'), *the*, 3; et, *and* 3; que (rel. pro.) *that, which*, 3; il *(impersonal) it, there*, 3; être, *to be*, 2; ne . . . pas, *not*, 2; du, des, *of the*, 2; de, *any*, 2; du, des, *some*, 1, de, *with*, 1, à, *at*, 1; mon, ma, mes, *my*, 1; son, sa, ses, *his, her, its*, 1; votre, *your*, 1;

pour, *as for*, 1; il fait du vent, *it is windy*, 1; il doit être, *it must be*, 1;—and so on with the rest of the items that have a single occurrence.

Some may object that the complexities of language learning are too great to be reduced artificially and mechanically to such simple terms as are indicated by the process outlined above. Language is, in fact, as complex as life and thought. But any definite planning is a gain. The attempt here is merely to find, in the complexity, a place to begin, and an order of progression.

It cannot be urged too strongly that there is no suggestion of translation in the sense of connected passages or even of invariably complete sentences. An attempt to simplify German word order, for instance, would demand typographical complexities altogether impractical. The recommendation is for learning units as units, and nothing more. In learning the unit *feu mon père* nothing needs to be added. But if and when a few units do happen to be combined, typographical devices may aid in preventing such silly, but actual, errors as "fire my father." The usual translation exercise which adds unit to unit without any specification encourages precisely this idiocy. When a unit is once learned, no further difficulty occurs. The child learning to read in the vernacular has a fund of language knowledge acquired before he sees its graphic representation. A tremendous confusion has been caused by beginning with an application of language to literature or thought and not with the units of which the language itself is composed. To specify connected material at the beginning of learning is to specify precisely that confusion.

WORD COUNTS

A determination of what choice to make of the infinite materials of a language demands first of all frequency counts of the units of expression. It is a remarkable fact that, in spite of the vast literature on methodology, the first word counts date back only a few years, and much work remains to be accomplished. According to Bagster-Collins,[2] one of the earliest studies, if not the earliest, in word frequencies was made by Professor H. C. Bierwirth in 1900. The Henmon French word count dates from 1924. The count of the Modern Foreign Language Study was not published until late in 1929.

An unfortunate feature of these estimates is that words have been chosen as the basic unit, rather than units of expression. As has been shown, the question of the language unit is at the bottom of much confusion concerning paradigms, word lists and translation—that is, the very basic questions of language methodology. The division of language into words is often a mere graphic accident, and an

[2] In *Methods of Teaching Modern Languages*, p. 79.

impossible source of confusion. The supplementary studies of idiom frequencies, like those of Cheydleur, provide, to some extent, a corrective, but certain difficulties that affect the practical value of frequency counts are inherent in the failure to consider the units of expression.

This difficulty is revealed in an attempt to apply practically the results of the French count of the Modern Foreign Language Study. Sixty-nine items, including the articles, the commonest prepositions, and verbs, were not included, as being obviously, and on the basis of previous counts, the most important words in the language. The items omitted appear simple enough, but, practically, they involve great difficulties. *Aller,* for instance, appears as one form, but, in fact, it represents a minimum of 45 separate units. Counting only the different inflected forms, there are 374 items of varying degrees of importance in the first 69 words. In the next 100 words, there are 454 different forms, and in the first 500 words, over 2,000 verb forms alone, not counting verbs exactly like any others. *Bon* counts as one word, although it is two *(bonne); être*=45; *le*=4; *à* and *de* equal 3 each; the possessive pronouns represent at least 15 forms,—and so on.

In most of these cases it would be impractical and unnecessary to list each item separately, but it would be interesting to know the relative frequency of different regular constructions and tenses,—for instance, of *il dit* and *nous allassions*. Above all, it is necessary to avoid confusion concerning the magnitude of the problem. *Saut* and *scélérat* appear boldly as separate items, but *je vais, il fut*, and *ils ont eu* hide discreetly under *aller, être*, and *avoir*, and, curiously, do not count at all in the usual lists of the first hundred or five hundred words.

When differences of meanings or functions are added to the two or three thousand forms somewhat hidden in the first 500 words, the difficulties, or rather obscurities, are still further increased. Each preposition may have the conventional equivalents, no equivalents (i.e. be omitted in the corresponding English unit) or be represented by any of a dozen or more English prepositions. Theoretically, ten words with ten different meanings each would permit 1,000 possible combinations. While no such extreme difficulty exists realistically, it is important to know which combinations, when there are any, and which meanings are most significant. *Sentir* means "to feel," but it also means "to smell," *grand* may mean "tall" or "large" or "great," *mettre* may mean "to place" or "to put on," *temps*, the time or the weather, and so on. Verbs like *aller* or *faire* may have columns of meanings in different units of expression and could offer a memory problem for weeks or months of study if no distinction were made between the frequencies of the different meanings. The first five hundred words represent

PROBLEMS AND IMPLICATIONS 179

perhaps thousands of semantic variations in addition to the two or three thousand inflectional forms. The practical difficulties are not so great, of course, as these figures indicate, but it is obvious that *faire* needs to be counted otherwise than *coton* or *corridor*.

In the actual count of the items, the failure to consider the units of expression introduces inevitably some confusion or error. In the word count in question, *par* counts as a unit, *par ici* either is not counted at all or counts twice, i.e., both for *par* and for *ici*. *N'en pouvoir plus* (to be exhausted) is most certainly a unit, but counts for the negative *ne,* for *en,* for *pouvoir* (to be able) and for *plus* (more, no more, no longer). *Faire faire quelque chose* counts twice for *faire*. *Vous avez beau le faire* (it is useless for you to do it) counts for the conventional equivalents of *have, beautiful,* and *to make.* *Il vient de parler* (he has just spoken) counts for *comes, of,* and *to speak.* These difficulties could be multiplied almost endlessly.

In the Modern Language Study count, an attempt was made in certain cases to distinguish between different words, e.g., *parler* (v.) and *parler* (n.), but this was done only in a very small proportion of the cases. A few phrases or units were listed separately, and others not. For example, *bien que* (although) is listed separately, but *à moins que* (unless) counts for *à, moins,* and *que*. *Aussi* (as), *aussi* (also), and *aussi* (therefore) were listed separately, but *coup,* which has several meanings, was not. This listing of a few items in combination and others exactly parallel as separate words probably caused some inaccuracy in the counting. For instance, *endormir,* used transitively in the sense of putting someone to sleep, has a range of 17, frequency 32; *s'endormir* (to go to sleep), which is certainly of much greater actual frequency, has a range of only 20, and a frequency of 37. *Aussitôt* (immediately, at once) has a range of 48, frequency 127, while *aussitôt que* (as soon as) a range of only 8, frequency 11, that is, just equivalent to *polonais* and *moucher* and less than *soutane, écorce, clôture,* and *abasourdir. Pendant que* (while) has less frequency than *preuve* or *verre.* These criticisms of detail might be continued, but the important point is the obscurity of the meanings of the most important items.

From a practical viewpoint, the frequency of occurrence of particular meanings of given words is of the utmost importance. It means almost nothing to say that *faire* equals "to make," "to go," "to have," "to be," etc. The important point is how many times it means "to be" and how many times "to make." Palmer cites the English word *"get,"* which may mean, (1) to grow or become, (2) to fetch, (3) to arrive at or reach, (4) to persuade, as in "get him to come"; (5) to cause to be *(get it mended),* (6) to make *(get it ready)* and (7) to receive *(I got a letter this morning)*. Such words need certainly to be listed separately for each meaning.[3]

Although the present word counts are defective in several respects, in the case of the less important items, they furnish essentially definitive information. The importance of such items as *épingle, turc,* or *mardi,* is definitely established. It may be possible through supplementary studies to determine the frequency of semantic variations of the most important items, and to combine with the word counts the results of the studies of idiom frequencies. It is mere justice to point out, morever, that word counts represent almost the first scientific and objective approach to problems of language study.

THE USE OF WORD COUNTS

In using word counts as a basis for the material of an elementary text, a distinction between words is necessary, not only on the basis of relative frequency but on the basis of relative difficulty as well. For example, the fifth most frequently occurring noun in French is *doute,* which scarcely needs presentation in an elementary text, since its meaning, in context, is immediately recognizable. In a straight running count, many words need almost no attention. The difficult words, on the other hand, may count toward reading knowledge as seven or eight, since

[3] *The Scientific Study and Teaching of Languages,* pp. 90, 91.

they may supply the key needed for understanding an entire sentence. The demand for drill on a given word depends, therefore, both on its importance and its difficulty.[4]

IMPLICATIONS OF THE RESTRICTED PROGRAM

Although the first postulate of the proposed program merely specifies the material to be learned and the order of learning it, a number of questions arise. Does learning units of expression mean learning the language? Is learning a language learning by heart? How about the childlike procedure, "ergonic combination," rules of grammar?

An apology for so simple a statement of the scope of the beginning course lies in the attempt to find a small common ground of possible agreement. It is doubtful if a smaller aim could be stated, or one that would unite a larger body of opinion. But even here certain implications have far-reaching effects.

Some use of the vernacular in defining the units is probably implied. That would not be the case if words or units could be chosen in any order, but the principle of frequency will hardly permit the degree of attention to names of concrete objects, e.g., *cahier, tableau noir, pupitre,* etc., that is almost nec-

---

[4] Certain experiments reported in the Appendix are intended to measure the relative difficulty of various classes of words that compose the French vocabulary.

essary in the beginning stages of exclusively oral methods. The principle of frequency cannot be applied with mathematical exactness, of course, but it would seem impossible or very difficult to explain the meaning of such words as *peu, falloir, alors, seul, jusqu'à ce que, devenir, en, comme,* etc.,—that is, the very words that are most important—to students who know no French whatever, without the use of the mother tongue.

Fortunately, this situation will hardly cause dismay. It is impossible to avoid translation in any case. Palmer devotes many pages to this subject. He points out how impossible a procedure it would be to develop anew definitions or concepts represented by words in frequent use:

> Thousands of our monologs and tens of thousands of our polylogs stand for most complex concepts and conceptual relations. . . . Let the reader imagine a case of complete aphasia or loss of memory and then let him realize the period of time and the amount of reading and study that would be required in order to re-form his associations. . . . We have learnt, let us say, mathematics, chemistry, or geology in our own language; we wish to read up or refer to works on these subjects written in some foreign non-cognate language. Are we, then, to study these sciences anew *ab ovo* in order to avoid the pernicious act of consulting the bilingual dictionary?

Let there be no illusion on this point; the most fervent partisan of the Direct Method translates, whatever his impressions to the contrary may be. He learns German by reading German books without a dictionary. He is reading a technical book dealing with chemistry; the word *Wasserstoff* occurs repeatedly. Our reader does not refer to a bilingual dictionary, it is true, but in the end he says to himself: 'Ach so, das Wort Wasserstoff bedeutet sicher *hydrogen!*'[5]

In the case of such words as *castor* (beaver), *hêtre* (beech), etc., unless a class is transferred to a woods or a zoo, the most ingenious efforts at designation will ultimately lead to the English equivalent. In the case of abstract concepts, the difficulties are equally great.

But if translation is used, it may resemble very slightly the old variety, certain classical examples of which have been cited. If English exercises occur (and, on these points, there is no attempt to decide the issues) they can serve merely to specify the foreign unit the student is to learn and to practice using. Their justification will probably depend in part on their value in enforcing attention, and in giving the student something to *do* rather than something to contemplate.

In respect to definition, if the principle of the unit of expression is carried out, *faire beau, faire un tour,* and *faire faire* will appear as different semantic items and be learned separately. In cases where a word has two or three meanings not neces-

[5] *The Scientific Study and Teaching of Languages,* pp. 90, 91.

sarily bound up with the context, it will appear once for each meaning, the most frequent meaning first, perhaps among the first hundred items, another meaning a thousand items farther on, and still other meanings lost in the lower frequencies. The advantage in clarity is obvious, and if experimental conclusions in associative inhibition can be applied to these cases, a very close bond with one primary meaning will make easier later associations with other meanings.

THE CHILDLIKE FACILITY

The apparent or real marvels of child learning have caused a desire to generalize the process. It is very likely that for an active use of the language, and with various classes of pupils, certain procedures that imitate child learning might prove the most effective. The program suggested in this book excludes no methods but it is concerned with studial learning, rather than with unconscious or "natural" learning.

On this point, not directly pertinent, the following observations occur:

Even casual observers have noticed the ease with which children learn to speak, the ultimate perfection of their sounds, and how parents with all their plans and conscious efforts, are out-distanced. Many explanations have been offered. In respect to pronunciation, a point not often mentioned is that the spoken language of any given region is merely a development that baby talk has reached. The adult population that imposes its speech learned that speech as children, and the stage of development represents a natural evolution that each new generation makes in common with the old. A child starts at a certain point and gets to a common ground, since the conditions are the same. The adult foreigner is in quite a different situation. His evolution of speech, in common with that of his ancestors, has led to different habits that are extremely difficult to change. The same difficulty exists in the case of most habits and muscular skills. An expert hockey player is helpless with a golf club precisely because of his excellence in the other game. Here a fact and a situation must be faced.

Some disproportion in judgment has been caused by the undue attention paid to sounds and accent, as apart from sense and understanding. There is no speech or accent admirable in itself. If the speakers of "Pennsylvania Dutch" or of Milt Gross' dialect replaced the natives in numbers and influence, their speech would become the standard. Almost everyone prefers his own sounds, and if an accent is ever absurd or unpleasant, it is largely because people dislike variations from group standards. Children and the uncultured are peculiarly intolerant. Kipling mentions how Stalky and Beetle carefully *kicked* McTurc out of his Irish dialect. A Frenchman once complained of "the inconceivable English pronunciation which defies the laws of human articulation." An Englishman might answer *tu quoque*. A course on French sounds may be considered, according to the viewpoint, as training in the defective habits of Parisian articulation.

The advantage of the child is limited. He has almost nothing to say, but his skill in saying it imposes. It would be unfortunate to allow a disadvantage that can't be helped to obscure other important advantages, to universalize the childlike procedure, and to follow in these matters popular influences and atavistic judgments.

COMBINATION OF THE UNITS

A question may arise as to whether a student can learn a language either actively or passively by memorizing detached and separate units. The answer is that the units are, by definition, those elements that can be combined. If a student learns "I have" and "a book" as separate items it is inconceivable that he could not say "I have a book." Yet the insistence on complete sentences is so general among writers on methodology that one wonders, after having investigated the evidence, what confusion is the source of this viewpoint. It is perhaps the same confusion noted everywhere between semantic units and words. If units could not be combined most speech would be impossible, and certainly the variations on M. Jourdain's famous verse, "Belle marquise, etc. . . . ," would be unintelligible.

SOME SUGGESTED EXPERIMENTS

A slight acquaintance with experiments in economy of learning will reveal the extraordinary possibilities for reform in language teaching. At present there is almost no concrete information available on the simplest questions that are faced by every writer who presumes to compose a text. No one knows how vocabulary should be presented, whether words should be grouped according to gender, meaning, or difficulty, how the pages should look, what kind of exercise is effective and for what purposes, how words should be defined, and so on. These are primary and fundamental matters of vital importance from every viewpoint except that, perhaps, of mental and moral discipline. Instead of experiment, there has been rationalizing and speculation.

The viewpoint here is that experimentation should begin, not with an attempt to verify a general theory, but with small specific problems. When information is available on many small points, the "methods" can take care of themselves.

The following topics are merely samples that will suggest other problems:

1. The economy of organization of material. The advantage or disadvantage of keeping words of a kind together. Arrangements by parts of speech, synonyms and antonyms, gender, difficulty, and so on, as compared with a mixed order of presentation.

2. The economy of rules as compared with learning inductively or by analogy. The degree of complexity which makes a rule ineffective. (Such rules as those for open and close vowels in Italian that permit a

multiplication of exceptions might serve as a guide in designing experiments under this heading).
3. The effect of context, of various kinds of context, of familiar and unfamiliar contextual words.
4. The economy or waste of abbreviated paradigms as compared with a complete presentation of all forms.
5. Typographical devices; arrangements of forms; use of bold face and italics for emphasis.
6. A comparison of particular devices for particular purposes with particular age groups. The inventions of the Gouin method, Pelmanism, the system of Hugo, etc. Such details as the various verb paradigm arrangements in use.
7. The effect of interlinear or other forms of translation (cf. the Harrap series) on rapidity of learning and retention.
8. The economy of suggesting associations, of devices to insure attention, of blanks, copying, questionnaires in the text, and so on.

In these experiments it will not be possible to discover in an absolute fashion the "best" form of presentation, since the possibility of invention of new devices will remain. But it should be possible to determine the relative advantage of different ways of presenting certain specific materials. With a body of information available on these points, the question of general method can be largely ignored, like the mental activities that preceded the founding of other sciences.

APPENDIX

EXPERIMENTS IN LEARNING WORD-PAIRS

§1
THE RELATIVE DIFFICULTY OF WORDS

The purpose of this experiment was to determine the relative difficulty of different classes of words. As a basic study, the first 50 words of each series of 500 words in the Modern Language Study French Word Count were classified roughly into five groups. The first group contained only words without obvious logical (or other) associations, e.g., *peu, alors, demain,* etc. The second group contained words that admit of logical associations with fairly common English words, e.g. *dent* (dentist) tooth; *glace* (glacier) ice, etc. The third and fourth groups contained words similar to English equivalents, graded according to degree of similarity, e.g., (class 3) *temps,* time; *loi,* law; *valeur,* value; (class 4) *incertain,* uncertain; *qualité,* quality; *rapidité,* rapidity, etc. The fifth group contained words exactly like the English equivalents (not counting accents or regular variations in feminine forms), e.g., *direction, rose, humble, expérience,* etc.

Because of the individuality of each word and inevitable subjective variations, the classification could only have an approximate accuracy, but it serves to indicate, certainly in a very general way, the character of the words that constitute the memory problem.

The percentage of words according to the various classifications is as follows:

I	II	III	IV	V
29%	17%	12%	27%	14%

From a practical viewpoint, and considering only recognition knowledge, the last two classes might be combined, since no student familiar with the vernacular equivalent would fail to recognize their French forms. They comprise 41 per cent of the French vocabulary, and can be excluded generally from the learning problem. The remaining 59 per cent of the words constitute the actual learning task. The first experiment was to determine the relative difficulty of words of the first three classifications.

Materials: In all the experiments, nonsense words were used in order to provide strictly comparable lists, and to avoid the possibility of direct or indirect acquaintance with the forms. In constructing the nonsense words, the consonants q and x were excluded, and the letters were used roughly in relation to their actual frequency. For instance, the consonants r, s, l, and t, were used more frequently than k, v, or z, and likewise, the vowel e was used oftener than u, and y was excluded. The words were usually formed vertically, i.e., a series of consonants would be written vertically, and the vowels supplied at random so that the resultant list represented a purely mechanical construction. Meanings were supplied according to the principle of the classification mentioned. List 1 offered no very obvious associations; in list 2, the meanings admitted associations as in the classification above, e.g. NADE (nude) bare; LETU (lettuce) salad, etc. The associations, however, were not suggested. In the 3d list, meanings were supplied that bore some resemblance in sound to the equivalent, e.g., JELOZ, jealous; RIZE, rice, etc. Two lists were used for words with logical associations in order to make possible a later comparison of the effect of suggesting or not suggesting the association link (see Experiment II).

The lists were as follows:

List 1A: MATU, barn; TEGO, fly; TUSI, jewel; JEDO, destiny; MUJO, anvil; TOGE, handle; MESI, bottle; NIMU, cloud; RAME, buzzing; NUKA, kitchen; GEPA, saddle; KIWA, spur.

List 1B1: LETU, salad; POKE, game; NADE, bare; NALA, wire; VOLU, bombardment; VARE, different; BOLA, dish; KARE, slowly; SUGE, white; LIPU, red; DURU, hard; LAMU, wool.

List 1B2: GOLA, end; JAMU, sweet; LULE, song; PETU, oil; JIPA, fortune teller; RUGE, red; ROKE, tool; LUNI, crazy; DUNI, mountain; RULO, ball; KOLU, drink; SUBO, mine.

List 1C: FALU, to fail; GELA, gelatin; KOBE, cob; LIMI, limit; LIPE, like; NUFO, enough; RIZE, rice; SENA, scene; TABO, table; VACA, vacant; WILU, willing; KOTE, coast.

Subjects: Four subjects were used in most of the experiments, Helen, age 12, a pupil in the 6th grade; Dorothy, age 14, a pupil in the second year of high school; a colored servant girl (Inez), age 16, who had been to high school and studied a foreign language, and Ch. a bilingual adult (age 30). The experimenter replaced Inez in later experiments when possible, since the number of repetitions required in her case would have introduced an element of fatigue for the same amount of work not present in the other cases.

Experimental method: The words with their English equivalents were presented on cards, exposed three seconds at each repetition, and presented both for learning and recall in mixed order (to eliminate the effect of position and learning by series). Tests were for immediate recall, and for recall after 24 hours.

Results

NUMBER OF REPETITIONS FOR IMMEDIATE RECALL

Subject	1A	1B1 or 1B2	1C
Ch.	8	2	2
Dot.	5	2	2
Helen	5	3	1
Inez	12	4	3
	30	11	8

APPENDIX

NEW REPETITIONS FOR DELAYED RECALL

Subject	1A	1B1 or 1B2	1C
Ch.	1	0	0
Dot.	0	0	1
Helen	1	1	0
Inez	3	2	1
	5	3	2

NO. OF WORDS REMEMBERED PER REPETITION AFTER 24 HOURS

Subject	1A	1B1 or 1B2	1C
Ch.	1⅓	6	6
Dot.	2⅙	6	5½
Helen	1⅓	3⅔	6
Inez	5/12	1½	3⅓
Average	1¼	4	5⅜

A record was kept of the responses for each word pair to determine whether any pair offered an especially large and consistent difficulty for all subjects. No such effect was revealed; the difficulties varied in individual cases.

Conclusion: In interpreting the results, it should be noted that only recognition knowledge is involved, that is, the ability to give the familiar equivalent of the unfamiliar term. The score for delayed recall is less significant than that for immediate learning, since the harder the list and the more repetitions, the greater is the amount of over-learning of certain items, and the difficulty of the delayed recall is proportionately reduced. In delayed recall a new repetition was required if only one item were forgotten, and, in general, the ease of learning made the duration of the impression relatively slight.

It is very probable that the absolute difficulty of the words used in the test is greater than that of actual words belonging to the same classes, because of the uniformity of the nonsense words. An experiment with real words showed this to be the case. But the extreme individuality of real words, and the variety of the subjective reactions to them make comparisons very difficult and uncertain. The purpose of the experiment was not to test absolute difficulty of French words, but the relative difficulty of words formed strictly according to the basis of the classification.

The difference in difficulty, according to the number of repetitions required for immediate recall is shown by the ratio 30-11-8. It is safe to conclude that words of the first class, i.e., about 29 per cent of the total words in the French vocabulary, offer most of the difficulty of the language.

An interesting fact in connection with these tests is the capacity for acquirement of words that they revealed. One twelve-year-old subject learned 12 words of class III in one minute and twelve seconds of study (including time spent in recall), and knew all of the words after 24 hours. To learn 36 words that represent the difficulty of a working vocabulary of perhaps almost a hundred running words, only about 12 minutes were required in repetition and recall. Nothing like this result is possible in practice, of course, but the fact is interesting in showing the effect of controlled and intense concentration.

§2
EFFECT OF SUGGESTED ASSOCIATIONS

Purpose: The purpose of the following experiments was to determine the value of suggesting associations in the case of those words that admit of this treatment, as compared with not suggesting them. Ex. (actual cases) DENT, tooth; or, DENT (dentist) tooth. As has been shown, about 17% of the words in the French vocabulary come under this classification.

Materials: Lists of word pairs with and without association links. The same words were used as in lists 1B1 and 1B2 of experiment 1 (the results of the experiments were combined). The suggested associations were as follows:

List 2A: LETU (lettuce) salad; POKE (poker) game; NADE (nude) bare; NALA (nail) wire; VOLU (volley) bombardment; VARE (various) different; BOLA (bowl) dish; KARE (careful) slowly; SUGE (sugar) white; LIPU (lip) red; DURU (durable) hard; LAMU (lamb) wool.

List 2B: GOLA (goal) end; JAMU (jam) sweet; LULE (lullaby) song; PETU (petroleum) oil; JIPA (gypsy) fortune teller; RUGE (rouge) red; ROKE (rake) tool; LUNI (lunatic) crazy; DUNI (dune) mountain; RULU (roll) ball; KOLU (coca-cola) drink; SUBO (subway) mine.

Experimental method: In this experiment, and in all those that tested two different manners of presenting material, the same lists were presented to two subjects in one form and to the other two subjects in the other form. Likewise the order was changed, i.e., if subject A had list 1 *with* associations first, subject B had the same list *without* associations first. The plan of presentation was as follows: Ch., list 2A without associations, list 2B with assoations; Dot, list 2A with associations, list 2B without associations; Helen, list 2B without associations, list 2A with associations; Inez, list 2B with associations, list 2A without associations. In this way any possible difference in absolute difficulty between one list and the other, and any advantage in presenting a list first or last, were equated. The results, therefore, isolate the factor of the manner of presentation. Since both lists were presented to each subject in succession, even such variations as differences in learning efficiency from day to day were equated. The word pairs were exposed for 3 seconds each in mixed order for both learning and recall.

The scores made were as follows:

APPENDIX

RESULTS

NUMBER OF REPETITIONS, IMMEDIATE RECALL

Subject	With suggested Ass'n	Without suggested Ass'n
Ch.	2	2
Dot.	1	2
Helen	2	3
Inez	7	4
	12	11

In delayed recall (24 hours) the new repetitions required were (with suggested associations) Ch. 1, Dot. 1, Helen 1, Inez 1, total 4; (without suggested associations) Ch. 0, Dot. 0, Helen 1, Inez 2, total 3. The figures for delayed recall, as has been mentioned, are not particularly significant, since the harder the learning, the greater the attention or the longer the exposure. Delayed recall becomes, generally, easier in proportion to the difficulty of the form of presentation.

The results of this experiment are not conclusive. The totals were affected considerably by the unusual performance of Inez, who required seven repetitions of the list with suggested associations as compared with a combined total of 5 for the other three subjects. The difficulty of concentration and understanding in her case, and the evident fatigue the process caused in comparison even with Helen, a twelve-year-old subject, made her performance perhaps somewhat capricious. The other three subjects showed a ratio of 5 as compared with 7 repetitions in favor of the suggested associations, i.e., a net gain of 2, or 40 per cent.

In another experiment, two additional lists were prepared in which the possible associations were not so immediately obvious. The results were as follows:

NUMBER OF REPETITIONS, IMMEDIATE RECALL

Subject	With suggested Ass'n	Without suggested Ass'n
Ch.	3	4
Dot.	2	3
Helen	2	3
	7	10

For delayed recall the results were as follows: (with associations) Ch. 1, Helen 0, Dot. 0, total 1; (without associations) Ch. 1, Dot. 1, Helen 1, total 3.

The gain in suggesting the associations was consistent in each subject. The total saving was 3 repetitions, or a gain of 43 per cent. This figure correlates fairly closely with the gain of 40 per cent by the same subjects in the previous test.

Conclusion. Further experimentation with more subjects is necessary to establish definitely the advantage of suggesting associations rather than allowing the subject to form associations of his own. It would seem, however, that there is an advantage in doing this, and that the advantage is probably very great. Three subjects representing wide age differences showed the same consistent results. It is possible, however, that the method of exposure, i.e., for three seconds, favored the suggested associations, since the time interval allowed little scope for independent search for association words—but this fact, of course, would not affect learning considered from the time-saving standpoint alone. Another possibility is that associations formed independently may have greater permanency. The difference, however, would probably be very slight. The associations formed spontaneously, but with a certain loss of time and effort in thinking them out, were found to be often the same or very similar to those suggested. Other association links were obviously less logical and more capricious than those that could be worked out deliberately as memory aids.

In respect to ease of memorizing, taking the last group as a whole, 36 words were learned in about 9 minutes for recall after twenty-four hours.

§3

THE EFFECT OF ORGANIZATION OF THE MATERIAL

The purpose of the following experiment was to determine whether or not groupings according to difficulty, syntactical classification or meaning would facilitate the learning process.

Materials: In the first experiment, words of various parts of speech were used, five of which were difficult and 7 relatively easy (classes 1 and 3). The words used were as follows:

List 3A1: (hard words) TREC, to hear; MIJI, hen; DOLU, because; ZIKO, what; POZU, lamp shade—(easy words) BLAP, flap; VEBA, verb; MALE, man; ROWI, boat; FLER, flower; NOVE, new; GRUP, group.

List 3A2: (hard words) FROP, to see; WEFO, chicken; MAGE, therefore; ZEJA, when; PRAZ, bell—(easy words) MILU, mile; GLEV, glove; BLAT, flat; BUKA, book; CELO, cellar; DOSE, medicine; DORI, adore.

Experimental Method: In the organized form of presentation, the difficult words were grouped together in one column, in the unorganized form all the words were mixed in two columns, as is usually the case in lesson vocabularies. The complete lists were exposed for 36 seconds (3 for each word), and the words presented for recall were on separate cards in mixed order. As in the other experiments, the order and form of the presentation of the two lists was varied in the case of all subjects, so that differences in absolute difficulty between the lists were equated in the total results.

RESULTS

NUMBER OF REPETITIONS FOR IMMEDIATE RECALL

Subject	Organized Presentation	Unorganized Presentation
Ch.	2	2
Dot.	2	2
Helen	2	2
H.	2	2
	8	8

In the number of items recalled after the first repetition the organized form gave somewhat better results, i.e., 40 as compared with 35, for all subjects. In delayed recall there was no difference in the total number of repetitions required, but the number of items recalled on the first presentation was 38 for the unorganized form, and 35 for the organized. Several preliminary experiments on arrangements by difficulty had failed also to give any significant results.

In two later experiments it was thought that a facilitating effect of grouping might be revealed by excluding any easy words, which would have the effect of an increase in the quantity to be learned. In the first of these experiments, only nouns were used, but of three kinds, names of animals, of common household objects, and of abstract qualities. The lists were as follows:

List 3B1: SUF, lion; IROV, wolf; TEWAN, tiger; BIGA, fox.—EPAH, coffee pot; CAZ, stove; SEJE, broom; NUBAL, dish pan.—DES, justice; AMEK, truth; FIJI, honor; TOLEP, love.

List 3B2: AMON, leopard; FUVE, cat; MEL, bear; NIFAB, elephant.—GEP, sink; PAZA, tea kettle; ESAN, dust pan; RETIL, mop.—JOB, hatred; ISET, honesty; KUDI, falsity; TIVUS, devotion.

The lists were presented in the organized form on a single card in three groups clearly marked off by the spacing. In the unorganized presentation they appeared in mixed order in two columns. Differences in difficulty of the two lists were equated as usual in the total results.

NUMBER OF REPETITIONS FOR IMMEDIATE RECALL

Subject	Organized Presentation	Unorganized Presentation
Ch.	3	3
Dot.	4	4
Helen	2	3
H.	3	3
	12	13

In the number of items recalled after the first presentation, the unorganized form gave here slightly better results, i.e., 22 as compared with 20.

In a third experiment, the procedure was still further varied in an attempt to produce a greater variation. In this case all the words were difficult, and the classes were formed of nouns, adverbs and verbs. Words of the same group were presented on separate cards (12 seconds for each of 3 cards). In the unorganized form, three cards were used also, but the words were mixed. The test for recall was by single words in varied and mixed order as before. The lists used were as follows:

List 3C1: LECA, to run; MODA, to rise; DURA, to sit; PEBA, to ask.—BUF, here; NAS, quickly; TEV, above; CAK, outside.—VITEB, house; BELOK, pencil; RIWID, pepper; GAMEL, husband.

List 3C2: JIVA, to walk; CUPA, to fall; ROKA, to stand; KEFA, to answer.—GIG, there; TOG, slowly; FEN, below; LOM, inside.—SURAB, barn; LATAN, pen; WASEG, salt; MEDUN, wife.

NUMBER OF REPETITIONS FOR IMMEDIATE RECALL

Subject	Organized	Unorganized
Ch.	3	3
H.	3	5
Dot.	6	6
Helen	4	4
	16	18

In this test a rather notable difference appeared in the number of words recalled after the first repetition. In the case of organized presentation, 23; unorganized, 12. Only in the case of one subject, however, was there any difference in the number of repetitions required to learn the entire lists.

Conclusion: In experiments of this kind, slight differences can hardly be considered as significant, and the results show almost no advantage for either form of presentation. This result came as a decided surprise to the experimenter, who expected that a clear advantage of the organization might appear. It is possible that, with longer lists, the advantage would become evident, but it appears safe to conclude that in short lists no surprising gains can be expected from either one method or the other. These results confirm those of Laird, Remmers and Peterson[1] who found that when recall is unorganized, it makes little difference whether the impression is organized or not.

§4
LEARNING UNITS IN COMBINATION

The purpose of this experiment was to determine the effect of presenting words in context, as the term is used by language teachers, i.e., in sentences or phrases, instead of separately. The practical question involved is whether or not it is better to introduce an unfamiliar term in combination with other unfamiliar terms, when the criterion for memory is the ability to recognize the word separately or in varying combinations.

Materials: Eight nouns were used and four verbs. The position of the nouns could be shifted so as to form 12 different sentences. The words were as follows:

List 4A1: DUL, men; KAS, women; FER, people; GIT, we, us; KOLEF, like; SEGUL, hate; VIDOR, fear; RABEN, see; BEGI, cats; RAKI, dogs; TOPU, horses; SUVE, mice.

List 4A2: KEL, boys; BUV, girls; GIL, children; KOM, they, them; REMOL, follow; SAREP, hear; LINOK, love; BUGAB, dread; KETA, mules; PASI, cows; GITO, sheep; MOBI, lambs.

---

[1] "An Experimental Study of the Influence of Organization of Material for Memorization Upon Its Retention," *Jour. Exp. Psy.,* 1923, 6, 293-303.

As will be noted the different classes of words are slightly distinguished by length. The sentences formed were similar to the following: "We fear mice," "Dogs like men," "Men see us," etc.

Experimental method: In the context form, a complete sentence was written on a single card, e.g., GIT VIDOR SUVE, *we fear mice,* and exposed for 9 seconds. In the other form, the word pairs were exposed, four on each card, for twelve seconds. The reason for presenting a group of four words was to balance the possible effect of the symmetry of the sentences due to the regular variation in the length of the words. The test for recall consisted of twelve sentences formed with the twelve words as noted above and presented on separate cards in any order. The possible differences in difficulty in the lists were equated by the method previously followed.

Results
NUMBER OF PRESENTATIONS FOR IMMEDIATE RECALL

Subject	In context	Without context
Ch.	6	3
Helen	8	5
Dot.	5	4
H.	5	2
	24	14

In delayed recall, the differences were slight, but, as has been pointed out, the saving method in delayed recall does not serve to measure the ease of learning. The gain in immediate recall in favor of the word pairs is striking, i.e., a saving of 10 repetitions or 71 per cent.

In another experiment, the procedure was varied. Two words formed a phrase, e.g., EBETI LANO, *to receive the letter*. These were presented as complete phrases and as separate words (three seconds allowed for each word whether presented individually or in the 2-word combinations). In the test for recall, the same form was used as in the presentation until all were recalled, and then recall in the other form followed immediately. For example, if the phrases were presented first, the first recalls were in terms of the phrases, and another recall followed immediately for the individual words. If the individual words were presented, the recall was first in terms of individual words, then in terms of phrases.

The phrases used were as follows:

List 4B1: EBETI LANO, to receive the letter; AKEMI RIDU, to tell the story; IMOPI ZOPA, to drink the water; ADIMI SEVO, to fear the result; OGURI WAFU, to laugh at the clown; UBALI KEKO, to go up the stairs.
List 4B2: EPULI PUTO, to close the door; IVOGI VIME, to leave the house; USEBI MAGI, to know the lesson; OZEDI NESI, to write the book; OTAFI TURE, to see the animal; ARIMI BOLU, to owe the money.

Results

When Presented as Word Pairs

Subject	Repetitions to recall individual words	Additional repetitions to recall phrases
Ch.	8	0
H.	4	0
Dot.	3	0
Helen	3	0
	16	0

When Presented as Phrases

Subject	Repetitions to recall phrases	Additional repetitions to recall individual words
Ch.	2	7
H.	3	5
Dot.	3	4
Helen	4	5
	12	21

The results of this experiment, as can be seen, were extraordinary. When words are presented paired individually with their meanings, 16 repetitions suffice to learn them for recall either individually or in combination. When they are presented as phrases, a total of 33 repetitions are required to learn them individually. More *additional* repetitions are required to learn the words individually than are required in the other form to learn them either way. This result appears almost as a psychological curiosity. The results were consistent in all individuals. Ch. sensed such an inhibition in trying to recall the individual words that she had to be encouraged to continue the experiment. The combined results eliminate all possible differences between the lists presented, since the same lists were easy or hard only according to the form in which they were presented.

Conclusion: The results of this double experiment involved such great differences, that little doubt is possible as to the interpretation. If the intention is to memorize units of expression as units for recognition either singly or in varying combinations, the method of presenting them in a fixed unfamiliar context is extremely wasteful. It would be difficult to find two ways of presenting the same quantity of material that would show such striking differences.

Summary

1. A relatively small proportion of the French vocabulary offers an extremely large proportion of the difficulty. This fact relates directly to the practical application of information furnished by word counts. Some words, in spite of high frequency, need scarcely any attention for recognition knowledge. The importance of a word, i.e., the amount of attention and drill it demands, depends on both its frequency and its difficulty.

2. Foreign words which have association links with their conventional equivalents are more easily recognized than those that do not, and it is probable

that there is a gain in suggesting the association when it is not immediately obvious.

3. In short word lists, there is no striking gain from grouping of the words according to difficulty, grammatical classification or meaning when the recall is not similarly organized.

4. Presenting units of expression in combination with other unfamiliar units is extremely wasteful if the intent is to teach the meaning of these units separately or in varying combinations.

An incidental fact of considerable interest revealed by all the experiments, is the surprising ability shown in learning the meanings of difficult and unfamiliar words. The speed of learning reveals what might be possible in language study through a proper distribution of the effort and through measures to insure brief but intensive concentration.

BIBLIOGRAPHY

Achilles, E. M., "Experimental Studies in Recall and Recognition," *Arch. of Psy.*, XLIV (1920), 80.

Adams, H. F., "A Note on the Effect of Rhythm," *Psy. Rev.*, XXII (1915), 289-98.

——— "The Effect of Climax and Anticlimax Order of Presentation on Memory," *Jour. of Appl. Psy.*, IV (1923), 330-38.

Alford, G. R., "Position in a Memorized Series," *Jour. Ed. Psy.*, III (1911), 458-59.

Anderson, J. P., and Jordan, A. M., "Learning and Retention of Latin Words and Phrases," *Jour. Ed. Psy.*, XIX (1928), 485-96.

Angell, J. R., "Methods for the Determination of Mental Imagery," *Psych. Monog.*, 1910, pp. 61-107.

Atkins, H. G., and Hutton, H. L., *The Teaching of Modern Foreign Languages in School and University*, London, 1920.

Austin, S. D., "A Study in Logical Memory," *Am. Jour. Psy.*, 1921, pp. 370-403.

Bagley, W. C., *The Educative Process*, New York, Macmillan, 1905.

Bahlsen, L., *The Teaching of Modern Language*, Boston, Ginn & Co., 1905.

Bair, J. H., "The Practice Curve, a Study in the Formation of Habits," *Psy. Rev. Mon. Sup.*, No. 19, 1902.

Balban, A., "Ueber den Unterschied des logischen u. des mechanischen Gedächtnisses," *Zeit. für Psychol.*, 1910, pp. 356-400.

Bancals, des, J., "Sur les méthodes de mémorisation," *Année Psychologique*, VIII (1902), 185-204.

Barlow, M. C., "The Rôle of Articulation in Memorizing," *Jour. Exp. Psych.*, XI (1928), 306-12.

Barrows, S. T., "Experimental Phonetics as an Aid to the Study of Language," *Ped. Sem.*, 1916, p. 63.

Barton, J. W., "Repetition in Learning," *Ped. Sem.*, XXIX (1922), 285-87.

Bennett, F., "Correlations between Different Memories," *Jour. Exp. Psy.*, 1916, p. 404.

Binet, A., et Henri, V., "La mémoire des mots," *Année Psychologique*, I (1894), 1-23.

Bonsfield, W. R., *The Basis of Memory*, New York, 1928.

Book, W. F., and Lee, N., "The Will to Learn," *Ped. Sem.*, XXIX (1922), 305-62.

Boswell, F. P., and Foster, W., "On Memorizing with the Intention Permanently to Retain," *Am. Jour. of Psy.*, 1916, pp. 420-26.

Bovée, A. G., "Some Fallacies of Formalism," *Mod. Lang. Jour.*, 1923, pp. 131-44.

——— "An Indicated Effect of Oral Practice," *Mod. Lang. Jour.*, 1928, pp. 178-82.

Braunschausen, "Les méthodes d'enseignement des langues étrangères," *Rev. Psychol.*, III (1910).

Breul, K. H., *The Teaching of Modern Foreign Languages*, Cambridge Univ. Press, 1913.

Busemann, A., "Lernen und Behalten," *Zeit. f. Angew. Psychol.*, 1911, pp. 211-71.

Buswell, G. T., "A Laboratory Study of Reading of Modern Foreign Languages," Vol. II, *Publications of the American and Canadian Committees on Modern Languages*, New York, Macmillan, 1927.

C., H. O., "Modern Languages," *Educational Times*, 1919, pp. 142-43; 234-36.

Calkins, M. W., "Short Studies in Memory and in Association," *Psy. Rev.*, 1898, pp. 451-62.

───── "Association," *Psy. Rev. Mon. Sup.*, 1896, Vol. I, No. 2.

Clarahan, M. M., "An Experimental Study of Methods of Teaching High School German," *Ed. Series, Univ. of Missouri*, Vol. I., No. 6, 1913.

Cole, R. D., "Free Composition versus Translation into the Foreign Language," *Mod. Lang. Jour.*, 1927, pp. 200-6.

Coleman, A., *Teaching of Modern Foreign Languages in the United States*, New York, Macmillan, 1929.

Conrad, H. E., and Arps, G. F., "An Experimental Study of Economical Learning," *Am. Jour. Psy.*, XXVII (1916), 507.

Cuff, N. B., "The Relation of Overlearning to Retention," Nashville, Peabody College for Teachers, Contributions to Education, No. 43, 1927.

Dexter, E. F., "An Analysis of a First Year Spanish Vocabulary," *Mod. Lang. Jour.*, 1928, pp. 272-78.

Douglass, "Certain Phases of Memory," *Ped. Sem.*, 1927, p. 109.

Ebbinghaus, H., *Memory*, New York, Columbia Univ. Press, 1913.

Elkin, D., "Ueber den Einfluss des Rhythmus und des Tempos auf den Gedächtnisprozess," *Arch. f. d. Ges. Psychol.*, 1928, 64, pp. 81-92.

Epstein, I., *La pensée et la polyglossie*, Lausanne, Payot, (1916?)

Erickson, C. L., and King, I., "A Comparison of Visual and Oral Presentation of Lessons in the Case of Pupils from the Third to the Ninth Grades," *Sch. and Soc.*, 1917, pp. 146-48.

Escher, E., "The Direct Method of Studying Foreign Languages," Chicago thesis, 1928.

Esper, E. A., "A Technique for the Experimental Investigation of Associative Interference in Artificial Language Material," *Lang. Monog.*, 1925.

—— "A Contribution to the Study of Analogy," *Psy. Rev.*, pp. 468-87.

Fisher, A., "Modern Languages by Way of Esperanto," *Mod. Lang.*, 1921, pp. 179-82.

Fisher, V. E., "A Few Notes on Age and Sex Differences in Mechanical Learning," *Jour. Ed. Psy.*, XVIII (1927), 562-64.

Frey, M., and Guenot, H., *Manuel de langue et de style français*, Paris, Masson, 1926.

Fukuya, S. M., "An Experimental Study of Attention from the Standpoint of Psychological Efficiency," Univ. of Chicago dissertation, 1917.

Gates, A. I., *Elementary Psychology*, New York, Macmillan, 1925.

—— "Recitation in Memorizing," *Arch. of Psy.*, 1917, No. 40.

Giddeon, A., "The Phonetic Method in Teaching Modern Languages," *Sch. Rev.*, XVII (Sept., 1909), 476-79.

Gordon, K., *Meaning in Memory and Attention*, Univ. of Chicago Press, 1903.

Grinstead, W. J., "An Experiment in the Learning of Foreign Words," *Jour. Ed. Psy.*, VI (1915), 242-45.

Guilford, J. P., "The Rôle of Form in Learning," *Jour. Exp. Psy.*, 1927, pp. 415-23.

Hall, G. S., "Some Psychological Aspects of Language Teaching," *Ped. Sem.*, XXI (1914), 256.

Hamilton, F. M., "The Perceptual Factors in Reading," *Arch. of Psy.*, 1907, No. 9.

Handschin, C. H., *Methods of Teaching Modern Languages*, Yonkers-on-Hudson, N. Y., World Book Co., 1923.

Hawkins, C. J., "Experiments on Memory Types," *Psy. Rev.*, 1897, pp. 289-94.

Henri, Chas., *Mémoire et habitude*, Paris, 1911.

Henmon, V., "Relation Between Mode of Presentation and Retention," *Psy. Rev.*, 1922, pp. 79-96.

———"Relation Between Learning and Retention and Amount to be Learned," *Jour. Exp. Psy.*, 1917, pp. 476-84.

———"Measurements and Experimentation in Educational Methods," *Jour. Ed. Res.*, XVIII (1928), 185-94.

Holmes, D. T., *Teaching of Modern Languages*, Paisley, Gardner, 1903.

House, C. C., "An Experiment Involving the Laboratory Method," *Mod. Lang. Jour.*, 1926, pp. 348-55.

Hunter, W. S., "Learning, II. Experimental Studies of Learning," in *The Foundations of Experimental Psychol.*, Worcester, Mass., Clark Univ. Press, 1929, pp. 564-627.

Inglis, A., *Principles of Secondary Education*, Boston, 1918.

Jenkins, J. G., and Dallenbach, K. M., "The Effect of Serial Position in Recall," *Am. Jour. Psy.*, XXXVIII (1927), 285-91.

Jespersen, O., *How to Teach a Foreign Language*, London, 1917.
—— *Language*, N. Y., Henry Holt and Co., 1922.
Johnson, C. L., "Vocabulary Differences and Text Book Selection," *Mod. Lang. Jour.*, 1927, pp. 290-97.
Johnston, C. H., *High School Education*, New York, Scribner's, 1912 (Chapter XIV on Modern Languages by W. H. Carruth.)
Judd, C. H., and Buswell, G. T., "Silent Reading," *Supp. Ed. Monog.*, No. 23, 1922, Univ. of Chicago Press.
—— *The Psychology of Secondary Education*, Boston, Ginn and Co., 1927.
Katzaroff, D., "Le rôle de la récitation comme facteur de la mémorization," *Arch. de Psych.*, 1908, pp. 225-58.
Kelly, T. L., "An Association Experiment," *Psy. Rev.*, 1913, pp. 479-504.
Key, C. B., "Recall as a Function of Perceived Relations," *Arch. of Psy.*, XIII (May, 1926).
Kirkman, F. B., *The Teaching of Foreign Languages*, London, 1914.
Kirkpatrick, E. A., "An Experimental Study of Memory," *Psy. Rev.*, 1894, pp. 602-9.
Kirsten, M., "*Zur pädagogisch-psychologischen Grundlegung der neusprachlichen Reform*," *Die Neuren Sprache*, 1921, pp. 30-44.
Kittson, E. C., *Theory and Practice of Language Teaching*, Oxford Univ. Press, 1918.
Krause, C. A., *The Direct Method in Modern Languages*, New York, Scribner's, 1916.
Laird, D. A., "How the High School Student Responds to Different Incentives to Work," *Ped. Sem.*, XXX (1923), 358-65.

Laird, Remmers, and Peterson, "An Experimental Study of the Influences of Organization of Material for Memorization upon its Retention," *Jour. Exp. Psy.*, VI (1923), 294-303.

Lentz, E., "Zum psychologischen Problem 'Fremdsprachen und Muttersprache'," *Zeit. f. Päd. Psych.*, 1901, p. 409.

Libby, W., "An Experiment in Learning a Foreign Language," *Ped. Sem.*, 1910, pp. 81-96.

Lyon, D. O., "Relation of Length of Material to Time Taken for Learning, and Optimum Distribution of Time," *Jour. Ed. Psy.*, 1914, pp. 85-91; 155-63.

Mabai, S., "Effects of Repetition on Retention," *Jour. Exp. Psy.*, V (1922), 147 ff.

McGamble, E. A., "Three Variables in Memorizing," *Am. Jour. Psy.*, XXXIX (1927), 223.

McGeoch, J. A., "Memory," *Psy. Bull.*, XXV (Sept., 1928), 513-49.

McKee, P., "Teaching of Spelling by Column and Context Forms," *Jour. Educ. Res.*, 1927, pp. 246-55.

Methods of Teaching Modern Foreign Languages, by various authors, Boston, D. C. Heath and Co., 1893.

Meumann, E., *Psychology of Learning*, New York, 1913.

Meyers, G. C., "Some Correlations between Learning and Recall," *Jour. Ed. Psy.*, 1916, pp. 546-47.

Michaelis-Passy, *Dictionnaire phonétique de la langue française*, Berlin, 1897, p. 313.

Modern Language Instruction in Canada, 2 vols., Univ. of Toronto Press, 1928. (Publications of the American and Canadian Committees on Modern Languages).

Morgan, C., "Vocabulary Analysis of a Second Year Spanish Text," *Mod. Lang. Jour.*, 1926, pp. 427-30.

Morrison, H. C., *Practice of Teaching in Secondary Schools*, Chicago, 1926.

Netschajeff, A., "Psychol. Beobachtungen zur Frage über den fremdländischen Sprachunterricht," *Pädagogisch-Psychol. Studien*, IX, Nos. 1 and 2, 1908.

Norsworthy, N., "Acquisition and Retention," *Jour. Ed. Psy.*, III (1911), 214-18.

O'Brien, F. J., "A Qualitative Investigation of the Effect of the Mode of Presentation on the Process of Learning," *Am. Jour. Psy.*, 1921, pp. 249-83.

O'Grady, H., *The Teaching of Modern Foreign Languages by the Organized Method*, London, Constable and Co., 1915.

Oliver, T. E., "Suggestions and References for Modern Language Teachers," University of Illinois, School of Education, Bull., No. 18, Urbana, 1917.

Orata, P. T., *The Theory of Identical Elements, being a critique of Thorndike's theory of identical elements and a re-interpretation of the problem of transfer of training*, Ohio State Univ. Press, Columbus, O., 1928.

Ordahl, L. E., "Consciousness in Relation to Learning," *Am. Jour. Psy.*, XXII (1911), 158 ff.

Palmer, H. E., *The Scientific Study and Teaching of Languages*, London, Harrap, 1917.

——— *The Principles of Language Study*, London, Harrap, 1921.

Pan, S., "Influence of Context upon Learning and Recall," *Jour. Exp. Psy.*, 1926, pp. 468-90.

Pargment, M. S., "Effect on Achievement of Method Used," *Mod. Lang. Jour.*, 1927, pp. 502-12.

Parker, S. C., *Methods of Teaching in High School*, Boston, Ginn and Co., 1915.

Patterson, T. L., "Pedagogical Suggestions from Memory Tests," *Jour. Ed. Psy.*, 1918, pp. 487-510.

Pear, T. H., *Remembering and Forgetting*, London, 1922.

Pechstein, L. A., "Massed versus Distributed Effort in Learning," *Jour. Ed. Psy.*, XII (1921), 92-98.

Peterson, H. A., "Influence of Complexity and Dissimilarity on Memory," *Psy. Rev. Mon. Sup.*, No. 49, 1910.

―――― "Recall of Words, Objects and Movements," *Psy. Rev. Mon. Sup.*, No. 17, 1903.

Piéron, H., *L'Evolution de la mémoire*, Paris, Flamarion, 1910.

Pohlmann, A., *Experimentelle Beiträge zur Lehre vom Gedächtnis*, Berlin, 1906.

Pyle, W. H., "Repetition and Retention," *Jour. Ed. Psy.*, II (1911), 311-21.

―――― "Economical Learning," *Jour. Ed. Psy.*, 1913., pp. 148-58.

―――― "Concentrated vs. Distributed Practice," *Jour. Ed. Psy.*, 1914, pp. 247 ff.

―――― *Psychology of Learning*, Baltimore, Warwick and York, 1928.

Quantz, J. O., "Problems of Psychology of Reading," *Psy. Rev. Mon. Sup.*, II (1897), No. 1.

Reed, H. B., "Repetition of Ebert and Meuman's Practice Experiment on Memory," *Jour. Exp. Psy.*, 1917, pp. 315-46.

―――― "Associative Aids," *Psy. Rev.*, 25, 128-55.

―――― "The Essential Laws of Learning or Association," *Psy. Rev.*, XXXIV (1927), 107-15.

———"Part and Whole Methods of Learning," *Jour. Ed. Psy.*, XV (1924), 107-15.
Richardson, R. F., "The Learning Process in the Acquisition of Skill," *Ped. Sem.*, 1912, pp. 376-94.
Roback, A. A., and Groetsinger, M., "The Applied Psychology of Names," *Jour. Appl. Psy.*, IV (1920), 348-60.
Robinson, E. S., "Memory," *Psy. Bull.*, XXI (Oct., 1924), 569-91.
———"Relative Efficiencies of Distributed and Concentrated Study in Memorizing," *Jour. Exp. Psy.*, 1921, pp. 327-43.
Robinson, E. S., and Brown, M. A., "Effect of Serial Position on Memorization," *Am. Jour. Psy.*, XXXVII (1926), 538-52.
Ruch, T. C., "Factors Influencing the Relative Economy of Massed and Distributed Practice in Learning," *Psy. Rev.*, XXXV (1929), 19-45.
Russell, R. D., "A Comparison of Two Methods of Learning," *Jour. Ed. Res.*, 1928, pp. 235-38.
Sandiford, P., *Educational Psychology*, New York, 1928.
Schlüter, L., "Exp. Beiträge zur Prüfung der Anschauungs und der Uebersetzungs Methode bei der Einführung in einem fremdsprachlichen Wortschatz," *Zeit. f. Psych.*, 1914, pp. 1-114.
Scholtkowska, G., "Exp. Beiträge zur Frage der direkten und der indirekten Methode im Neusprachlichen Unterricht," *Zeit. f. Angew. Psych.*, 1925, pp. 65-87.
Schuyten, M. C., "Experimentelles zum Studium der gebräuchlichsten Methoden," *Zeit. f. Exp. Pädagogik*, 3 Bd., 1906.

Schweitzer, M., *Méthodologie des langues vivantes*, Paris, Colin, 1903.

Segal, J., "Ueber den Reproduktionstypus," *Arch. f. d. Ges. Psychol.*, 1908, pp. 124-35.

Seibert, L. C., "An Experiment in Learning French Vocabulary," *Jour. Ed. Psy.*, 1927, pp. 294-309.

Smith, M., and McDougall, W., "Some Experiments in Learning and Retention," *B. Jour. Psy.*, X (1919), 204 ff.

Smith, W. G., "Place of Repetition in Memory," *Psy. Rev.*, Vol. III (1896).

────── "Relation of Attention to Memory," *Mind*, New Series, Vol. IV (1895).

Starch, D., "Experimental Data on the Value of Studying Foreign Languages," *Sch. Rev.*, XXIII (1915), 697-703; XXV, 243-48.

Steffens, L., "Zur Lehre vom ökonomischen Lernen," *Zeit. f. Psychol.*, XXII (1900), 321 ff.

"Studies in Modern Language Teaching," Vol. XVII, *Publ. of American and Canadian Committees*, New York, Macmillan, 1929.

Sullivan, "Attitude and Learning," *Psy. Rev. Mon. Sup.*, Vol. XXXVI, No. 3.

Sweet, H., *The Practical Study of Languages*, London, Dent, 1899.

Swift, E. J., "Studies in the Psychology and Physiology of Learning," *Am. Jour. Psy.*, 1903, pp. 201-51.

────── *The Mind in the Making*, New York, 1906.

Swift, Z. O., "Beginning a Language," in *Studies in Phil. and Psy.* by former students of C. E. Gorman, pp. 297-313.

Symonds, P. M., "Laws of Learning," *Jour. Ed. Psy.*, 1928, pp. 405-28.
Thorndike, E. L., "Repetition vs. Recall in Memorizing Vocabulary," *Jour. Ed. Psy.*, 1914, p. 596.
────── *Educational Psychology* (briefer course), New York, 1924.
────── *The Psychology of Arithmetic*, New York, 1923.
────── *Educational Psychology*, Vol. II. *The Psychology of Learning*, Columbia Univ., New York, 1926.
────── "Memory for Paired Associates," *Psy. Rev.*, 1908, pp. 122-38.
────── "Memory for Words and Numbers," *Am. Jour. Psy.*, XXI (1910), 487-88.
────── Bregman, E. O., Tilton, J., and Woodyard, E., *Adult Learning*, New York, Macmillan, 1928.
Trow, W. C., "Recall versus Repetition in Learning of Rote and Meaningful Material," *Am. Jour. Psy.*, XL (1928), 112-16.
Washburne, J. N., "An Experimental Study of Various Methods of Presenting Quantitative Material," *Jour. Ed. Psy.*, XVIII (1927), 361-76; 465-76.
Watt, H. J., *The Economy and Training of Memory*, New York, 1909.
Webb, L. W., "A Comparison of Two Methods of Studying with Application to Foreign Languages," *Sch. Rev.*, 1921, pp. 58-67.
West, M., *Bilingualism*, Bureau of Education, Occas. Rep., No. 13, Calcutta, 1926.
Whipple, G. M., *Manual of Mental and Physical Tests*, Balt., Warwick, and York, Vol. II, 1915.

——— "The Transfer of Training," *27 Yrbk. Nat. Soc. Stud. Educ.*, Part II, 1928, 179-209.

Winch, W. H., "Immediate Memory in School Children," *Brit. Jour. Psy.*, Vol. I, Part 2, 1904.

Winzen, K., "Die Abhängigkeit der paarweisen Assoziation von der Stellung des besser haftenden Gliedes," *Zeit. f. Psychol.*, 1921, 86, pp. 236-52.

Witasek, S., "Ueber Lesen und Rezitieren in ihren Beziehungen zum Gedächtnis," *Zeit. f. Psy. u. Phys. d. Sinnes*, 1907, pp. 161-246.

Wohlgemuth, A., "Simultaneous and Successive Association," *Brit. Jour. Psy.*, VII (1915), 434-52.

Wood, I., "A Comparative Study of Vocabularies of Sixteen French Texts," *Mod. Lang. Jour.*, 1927, pp. 263-89.

Woody, C., "Effectiveness of Oral versus Silent Reading in Initial Memorization," *Jour. Ed. Psy.*, XIII (1922), 477-83.

Worcester, D. A., "Retention by Visual and by Auditory Presentation," *Jour. Ed. Psy.*, XIV (1923), 113 ff.

——— "Memory by Visual and Auditory Presentation," *Jour. Ed. Psy.*, XVI (1925), 18-27.

Young, C. E., and Daus, J. M., "An Experiment in First Year French," *MLJ*, 1928, pp. 356-64.

Young, C. E., and Vander Beke, G. E., "An Experiment in Second Year French," *MLJ*, 1927, pp. 25-31.

Zuccari, G. R., "Ricerche sulla importanza dei movimenti articolatori," *R. di Psicol.*, XI (1915), 187-95.

INDEX

ACCENT, 114, 186
Achilles, E. M., 54
Adams, H. F., 68, 72
Age, 74 ff., 77
Ahn, 101, 102, 103, 113
Aims, 124 ff., 129
American Council Tests, 75
Anderson, J. P., 60
Arithmetical fallacy, 87
Arnold, 103
Articulation, 68 ff., 77, 117
Association, 25, 29, 39, 50 ff., 76, 96, 189, 199 ff.
Association Phonétique, 82, 98, 105, 113, 114
Associative Inhibition, 72 ff.
Assonance, 77
Atkins, H. G., 114, 116, 135
Attention, 70 ff., 77
Attitude, 61 ff., 77
Aural Approach, 111 ff., 155
Austin, S. D., 62, 63
Awtry, H., 121

BABBITT, E.H., 131
Bagley, W. C., 55, 65, 99
Bagster-Collins, E. W., 20 n., 82, 102 n., 104, 144, 158, 176
Bahlsen, L., 85
Bain, A. W., 142
Balban, A., 50, 96
Barlow, M. C., 68
Berlitz Schools, 155
Bierwirth, 176
Bilingualism, 135 ff.
Binet, A., 41, 69, 70, 97
Blackburne, M., 159
Bonsfield, W. R., 52
Book, W. F., 62
Boswell, F. P., 61
Bovée, A. G., 14, 17

Braunschausen, 28, 29, 31, 34, 38
Breul, K., 82, 88, 104, 108, 116, 144
Breymann, H., 140
Brown, H. H., 115
Buseman, A., 50
Buswell, G. T., 35, 37 n.

C——, H. O., 83, 86, 89, 113, 115, 126, 158
Calcutta Univ. Comm., 144
Calkins, M. W., 53, 64
Canadian Committee, 14, 20, 32, 41, 46, 62, 68, 75, 86, 96, 98, 103, 105, 111, 121, 125, 127, 135, 140, 144, 146, 160, 161
Carr, W. L., 58
Cerf, B., 144
Cheydleur, F. D., 20 n., 177
Churchman, P. H., 144
Clarahan, M., 12
Colbeck, C., 121, 144
Cole, R. D., 37
Coleman, A., 14, 21, 37, 59, 68, 75, 121, 125, 142, 143, 157 n., 159 n.
Combination of units, 187
Completion exercises, 106
Complexity and dissimilarity, 53 ff.
Composition, 101 ff.
Context, 27, 28, 38, 50 ff., 96 ff., 154, 189, 208 ff.
Counts of frequency, 174, 176 ff.

DALLENBACH, K. M., 70
Daus, J. M., 67
Designation of units, 171
Difficulty of words, 193, 198
Direct association, 37, 39

Direct method, 16, 33, 34, 36, 94 n., 129, 140 ff., 183
Direct reading method, 37
Direct values, 125
Dissimilarity, 53 ff.
Distribution of learning, 62 ff., 77
Douglass, H. R., 47 n.
Drill, 64 ff., 77, 110, 182

EBBINGHAUS, H., 47, 48, 60, 61
Elkin, D., 68
English exercises, 105, 109, 155, 184
Epstein, I, 139
Exercises, 105, 109, 155, 184
Experimental results, 149
Experiments suggested, 187
Eye movements, 35

FOSTER, W., 61
Free composition, 101 ff.
Free translation, 37
Frequency counts, 174
Frey, M., 151 n.
Fukuya, S. M., 71 n.

GALLI, A., 54
Gates, A. I., 55, 60
Gordon, K., 53, 63
Gouin method, 156, 189
Grammar, 82 ff., 151
Grammar-translation method, 16, 19, 37, 89, 107, 148
Grandgent, C. H., 133
Greenup, J. C., 18
Grinstead, W. J., 38, 41
Groetsinger, M., 72
Guenot, H., 151 n.
Guilford, J. P., 66

HABIT formation, 99, 152
Hagboldt, P., 88
Hamilton, F. M., 96, 97
Handschin, C. H., 4, 11, 14, 22, 28 n., 38 n., 41, 44, 124, 128
Harrap Series, 189
Hawkins, C. J., 45
Henmon, V. A. C., 45, 67, 158, 176
Hootkins, C. J., 45
Hugo System, 156, 189
Hunter, W. S., 49
Hutton, H. L., 114, 116

IMAGERY, 75
Incidental learning, 99
Indirect bond, 94 n.
Indirect method, 33 ff., 36, 94 n.
Indirect values, 125, 157, 163
Inductive learning, 152
Inglis, A., 126
Inhibition, 72 ff.
Interest, 98, 154
Interference, 54 ff., 135 ff.
Interlinear translations, 189
Intonation, 116

JAMES, A. L., 116
Jenkins, J. G., 70
Jespersen, O., 86 n., 92, 112 n., 134, 136, 137
Jordan, A. M., 60
Judd, C. H., 20, 47, 121, 127

KAPPERT, H., 121
Katzaroff, D., 60
Kemsies, 45
Kirkman, F. B., 103, 109, 125, 145
Kirkpatrick, E. A., 22, 38, 39
Kirsten, M., 110, 141
Kittson, E. C., 89, 111, 112, 113

INDEX

Klemm, O., 51 n.
Kline, L. W., 73
Kuhlmann, 53

LAIRD, D. A., 66, 207
Language unit, 87 ff., 95, 153, 166 ff.
Laurie, 136
Lee, F., 62
Lentz, E., 139
Libby, W., 27, 41, 96, 98
Living speech, 111 ff., 157
Lodeman, A., 121
Loram, 137
Lyon, D. O., 62

McDOUGALL, W., 71
McGeoch, J. A., 48, 54, 72, 73
Mabai, S., 61
Mass experimentation, 150
Memorial capacity, 59 ff., 76, 198
Memory for objects, words, etc., 22, 24, 27, 29, 32, 34
Meter, 77
Methods, 11, 12, 16, 19, 31, 33, 36, 37, 39, 121 ff., 148, 155 ff.
Meumann, E., 44, 47, 52, 62, 64, 68, 70
Michælis-Passy, 82 n.
Mode of presentation, 44 ff., 75
Modern Foreign Language Study, 5, 14, 19, 36, 176, 177, 179
Monahan, F. J., 137
Morgan, B. Q., 87 n., 112 n.
Motor memory, 46
Müller, 50
Murphy, H. H., 62

NETSCHAJEFF, A., 29, 30, 31, 34, 38
Nonsense words, 150

OBJECT method, 22, 30, 31
Objectives, 121 ff., 155 ff.

O'Brien, F., 44 n.
Ollendorff, 102, 103, 113
Oral approach, 17, 111 ff., 143, 155
Ordahl, L. E., 70
Order of presentation, 71
Organization of material, 66, 77, 152, 188, 203 ff.
O'Shea, M. V., 142, 143

PALMER, H. E., 37, 88, 89, 90, 107, 110, 112, 121, 129 n., 164, 166, 168, 169, 180, 183
Pan, S., 52, 96
Panicelli, J. B., 61
Paradigms, 86 ff., 107, 153, 189
Pargment, M. S., 15
Parker, S. C., 115
Part and Whole methods, 47 ff., 76
Patterson, T. L., 133
Pelmanism, 156, 189
Peterson, H. A., 23, 28, 31, 34, 38, 39, 53, 54, 66, 207
Phonetics, 114 ff.
Picture method, 32, 93
Pinloche, A., 142
Pohlmann, A., 33, 35, 45
Position in series, 69
Prendergast, 103
Pronunciation, 114, 115, 186
Purin, C. M., 104
Pyle, W. H., 62, 63 n.

READING knowledge, 111, 144 ff., 147, 157, 162, 163
Reading method, 12, 19
Recall, 60 ff.
Reed, H. B., 49, 51
Repetition, 60 ff., 64 ff., 72, 77
Retroactive inhibition, 72 ff.
Rhythm, 68, 77, 116
Rice, W. F., 57

Rippmann, W., 82, 85
Roback, A. A., 72
Robinson, E. S., 48, 63, 70, 72, 73
Rockwood, R. E., 159
Ruch, T. C., 64

Saer, D. J., 135
Sallwuerk, 93
Sandiford, P., 55, 65, 70, 75
Sawdon, 48
Schlüter, L., 30, 34, 35, 37, 38, 39, 40, 93, 107
Schmidt, F., 130
Schoenherr, W., 32, 34, 38
Scholtkowska, G., 33, 34, 35, 38, 40
Schuyten, M. C., 26, 31
Sears, 159
Seibert, L. C., 68
Semantic differentiation, 171, 173, 174, 179
Sensory modality, 44
Sentence definition, 89, 153
Siepmann, O., 111, 114
Sigwalt, C., 142, 144
Skaggs, E. B., 73
Skelton, 138
Smedley, 46
Smith, F., 135
Smith, M., 71
Sounds, 186
Sparkman, C. F., 88
Speaking knowledge, 87, 112, 130 ff., 162, 163
Starch, D., 56
Stern, W., 139
Suchardt, 137
Sullivan, E. B., 61
Sweet, H., 85, 87, 88, 92, 95, 99, 103, 104, 108, 115, 130
Swift, E. J., 61
Symonds, P. M., 47

Tharp, J. B., 111 n.
Thomas, C., 121, 131, 132, 145
Thorndike, E. L., 55, 59, 65, 74, 75, 103, 126
Ticknor, G., 20, 83 n.
Transfer, 54 ff., 126
Translation, 101 ff., 106, 153, 155, 175, 182 ff.
Trow, W. C., 60, 63
Tsai, L., 63
Typographical devices, 76, 77, 109, 173, 189

Umbach, M. E., 141
Unit of articulation, 117
Unit of language (expression), 87 ff., 95, 109, 166 ff., 179
Units, designation, 171
Units, combination, 187, 208 ff.

Values of language study, 124, 125 ff., 156, 157, 163
Vander Beke, G. E., 67
Variations in memorial capacity, 59
Viëtor, W., 88
Vocabulary arrangements, 27, 29, 31, 32, 40
Von Sybel, 45

Washburne, J. N., 51 n., 66
Watt, H. J., 76
Webb, L. W., 60
Welch, G. B., 54
Werner, O. H., 56
West, M., 68, 93, 94 n., 112, 113 n., 114, 132, 133, 135, 137, 138, 146, 147, 162, 163 n.
Whipple, G. M., 44 n. 45, 56
Whitely, P., 73
Widgery, W. H., 103
Winch, W. H., 48

Winzen, K., 72
Witasek, S., 60
Wood, I., 159, 161
Woodworth, R. S., 52 n.
Woody, C., 58, 68
Worcester, D. A., 61
Word counts, 176 ff., 181 ff.

Word lists, 38, 92 ff., 101, 153
Wundt, W., 91

YOUNG, C. E., 67

ZUCCARI, G. R., 68

www.ingramcontent.com/pod-product-compliance
Lightning Source LLC
Chambersburg PA
CBHW021123300426
44113CB00006B/262